"To the thousands of people interested in and working with Small Christian Communities, here is a book from the long-distance people of vision to keep you going. *Forming Small Christian Communities: A Personal Journey* is a book of unusual wisdom and deep-hearted spirituality. Currier and Gram make present the vision of what human life and the church can look like, and where we surely should be heading. This book deserves to be read."

Rev. Art Baranowski
Director, National Alliance of Parishes
Restructuring into Communities

"This is the most practical book on starting, maintaining, and nourishing a small community that I have read. It's packed with practical, down-to-earth ideas and suggestions. The best part of the book are the "Questions and Answers" at the end of each chapter. The authors ask and answer some very tough questions, the very ones I hear most often about small groups.

"This book takes us beyond theory and theology into the world of actually *doing* small community life together. In lovely, gender-inclusive language and style, the authors offer a view of the church that is at once radical in leading the baptized to exercise their own priesthood, and honest in naming the pitfalls as that becomes a reality in our time. I'd like to put this book into the hands of everyone struggling to make small communities work."

Bill Huebsch
Theologian and Author
Minneapolis, Minnesota

"In *Forming a Small Christian Community: A Personal Journey*, Currier and Gram have woven a user-friendly blend of historical relationship, theoretical understanding, and practical instruction. As I read, I gained a deeper understanding of the history, nuances, and potential of my own small community and found myself responding, 'Yea...all-right!' as I recognized mutual experiences and challenges.

"Readers will discover that this book is a realistic tool whether they are beginning the 'exciting new venture' of SCC or are in the midst of the 'long haul' of community."

Barb Darling
Member of Oilers' SCC since 1971
Editor of Buena Vista Newsletter

"Richard Currier and Fran Gram offer a significant piece to the puzzle about how to foster small faith communities in the American culture of the late 20th century. Their advice is just *do it*! How refreshing. No elaborate plan, no dividing up the parish, no sign-up sheets, not even trained facilitators. Just *do it*!

"Suppose you're interested in a small faith community. You're not a priest, staff person, or pastoral council member. All you have to do is call together one or two neighbors or friends and start an informal dialogue over favorite scripture passages. It's as simple as that. The authors are not denying the role that parish leaders could play in forming small communities. It's just that you don't have to wait for them to get started. After talking with one another for awhile, call in more people and you're in business. You are a small Christian community, no further sanction needed. For this one reason alone, I recommend this book to as wide an audience as possible.

"The rest of the book takes the group through a growing awareness of its mission and purpose, centered around the roles of priest, prophet, and kingly servant. The priestly role is related to the group's experience of worship, the prophetic to calling into question current priorities in our culture, the servant role to loving and healing.

"Each chapter concludes with a series of questions and answers that help a group 'go deeper' into the meaning of small Christian communities. One answer concludes with a resounding statement about the effectiveness of the current small community movement in revitalizing the church today. 'To regain an effective voice in the rapidly changing world, the Catholic church is rediscovering its roots stemming from dialogue, the essential dynamic of the SCC. Throughout the world, small communities are emerging as a basic structure of the Catholic church, because it is only at this level that dialogue is possible.'" (p. 125)

Thomas P. Sweetser, S.J.
Parish Evaluation Project

FORMING *a* Small Christian Community

A PERSONAL JOURNEY

Richard Currier & Frances Gram

TWENTY-THIRD PUBLICATIONS
Mystic, Connecticut 06355

Twenty-Third Publications
185 Willow Street
P.O. Box 180
Mystic CT 06355
(203) 536-2611
800-321-0411

ISBN 0-89622-511-9
Library of Congress Catalog Card Number 91-68557

Contents

Introduction

Welcome aboard! You are about to embark on a journey that will enrich your life beyond your imagination. Picking up this small book that introduces you to small Christian community (throughout the book referred to as SCC) is an important first step toward embarking into a wondrous new world. You are headed for an uncharted new frontier, not one of mysteries in the open spaces above nor a probing of the secrets in the oceans below, but rather the last and greatest frontier of all, namely, you. A step into the mysteries of small Christian community is first and foremost the beginning of a journey into the most precious and exciting world of your own person. SCC is about you.

Something important is already going on within you at this very moment, something that has influenced you to make a decision to pick up this book. Your interest in SCC is like a tiny mustard seed (Matthew 13:31) that, if nurtured, will grow to become so large that others will be attracted to its shade.

While you read this book, we will be your guides, but when we part at the end of this book, you will, we hope, have a vision of yourself in the context of SCC that will transform your life with peace and joy.

SCC may be a charting of new waters for you, but you need not be afraid, because you are not alone. The Spirit of Christ has been at work within your heart and will continue to be your constant companion, as indeed the Spirit has led the whole church throughout the ages. Be assured that SCC, the exciting new venture growing rapidly throughout the world in the church of today, will lead you closer to Christ. SCC is evidence that the promised Spirit of Christ continues to abide in the church to gently but firmly recreate it to meet the needs of the modern world.

Bishop John F. Fitzpatrick of Brownsville, Texas, offered this message in a pastoral letter to his people. He wrote:

> In our time, the church is experiencing an exciting, world-wide rebirth in the form of small communities of faith. This is happening at a time when modern societies have produced huge structures and complex bureaucracies that have left people feeling anonymous, uprooted, and alienated....Ironically, it is the successful growth of Catholic parishes over time that has eventually made them also impersonal and unable to provide a sense of real community. The Vatican Council presented the church as a people, a communion, a discipleship of equals who celebrate life and live the gospel together. The success of base communities [SCC] has been a surprise to many. Their marvelous growth cannot be explained except by the outpouring of the Holy Spirit.

Bishop Fitzpatrick's words echo a statement made by the American bishops in 1987:

Conversion and a sense of being church are often best lived out in smaller communities within the parish, which are more personal and offer a greater sense of belonging. These small ecclesial communities and other groups within the parish framework promote experiences of faith and conversion, prayer life, missionary outreach and evangelization, interpersonal relations and fraternal love, prophetic questioning and actions for justice. They are a prophetic challenge for the renewal of our church and humanization of our society.

As you begin your journey, you are in the company of thousands of other believers who struggle with the meaning of SCC. As your guides, our first admonition to you is that enthusiasm for the development of SCC in the church is not enough. You must approach SCC for the "long haul" with your eyes wide open. The purpose of this book is to provide you not only with a solid historical and theological foundation for SCC, but also a practical, step-by-step introduction to translate your initial interest into a realistic vision of what must be done.

Taking up this book is the first step. The second step toward implementing SCC in your life, or into parish life, is for you to clearly recognize and be convinced that SCC is indeed about you. SCC is not just another project or activity. Your growth in spirituality will bring about new life in the form of Christian community. In other words, SCC is not an organization to which you belong but an environment that enables you to grow to full maturity as a person grounded in faith, rooted in hope, and yielding the precious fruit of love. If this seems confusing, be patient because it will become evident as you progress on your journey.

This leads us to a third important point. It is essential to recognize that SCC is a process. In the Western world we are inclined to view the church in static terms as a hierarchical organization or as an aesthetically designed building where

Mass and the sacraments are celebrated. In SCC a static view of Christian community is not enough. People cannot be ordered to belong to SCC by hierarchical authority, but must be invited or attracted to it as a way of life. SCC is a "process" that is not restricted to Sundays, since it embraces the whole of life.

Process is a secular word for "dialogue" (in Latin: *communio*). This dialogical process is three dimensional: contemplative, insightful, and transforming. SCC leads to growth in contemplative prayer. As a person develops a prayer life, he or she will gain ever greater insight into the mysteries of the gospel and thus become a more mature Christian. Finally, the person involved in SCC will be transformed personally, and as a consequence will begin to transform society.

In sum, SCC is not so much what we do or accomplish in life, as what we become. Many have longed to see what we now see, but have been blind; many have longed to hear what we now hear, but have been deaf.

At the end of each chapter in this book there are questions and answers that focus on a variety of practical issues. These are not intended as catechism lessons. If we had all the answers, SCC would be very boring indeed. Thus this section is intended as an invitation to dialogue. Also, included at the close of each chapter is a series of discussion questions on the content of the chapter. These are for group use.

The pages that follow will tell much more about us than the brief words above because, it is hoped, they will give greater definition to the emerging SCC in the church today but also reveal who we are and what we hold precious.

Note: The term "small Christian community," as already noted, is always expressed as SCC; the plural as SCCs. When no modifier precedes SCC, it is understood to mean the singular indefinite, a small Christian community.

Chapter 1

In the Beginning

It is surprising how much we can learn about small Christian community (SCC) in the first chapters of Genesis, the first book of the Bible. In the opening chapters, God creates the heavens and the earth, the sea with its countless varieties of fish, the birds of the air and plants and animals on dry land. But when God makes Adam, God makes him as a friend after God's own image and likeness. The author of Genesis tells us that God took frequent walks with Adam, as you would expect two good friends to do, through the garden paradise God had made. The heart-to-heart dialogue is a source of great joy for both. So delightful is the dialogue that God determines that Adam should have another human being with whom to extend this dialogue. And so, God made Eve to be with Adam as a friend in his garden paradise.

In this beautiful account of the origins of the human race, the ancient writer sees the loving dialogue between God and the individual, extending to envelop the individual's dialogue with other human beings, as the centerpiece in a plan for all of the universe in which joy and harmony would reign supreme.

But the author of Genesis is not a dreamer and could plainly see that, far from dialogue and harmony, conflict and disharmony were everywhere. The author tries to give an account of what led to the turmoil. The conclusion is that Adam and Eve chose to have an exclusive friendship and make the wonderful world that God had made their own exclusive possession. They shut God out of the dialogue. The Genesis author then proceeds to unfold the consequences of Adam and Eve's decision in the story of Cain and Abel, their descendants. (See Genesis, Chapter 4.)

When Dialogue Is Disrupted

Cain was jealous of his brother Abel, and he murdered him. When God asked Cain where his brother was, Cain tried to cover his crime by rhetorically asking why he should be concerned about his brother. After all, was he his brother's keeper?

The author of Genesis, in writing about the origins of the human race, is expressing some profound truths in a most eloquent way. First and foremost is that the relationship with God was intended from the beginning to be that of a dialogue between friends in a universe paradise. Secondly, one's friendship with God is extended in the dialogue one has with other human beings, because we are all made to the image and likeness of God. Finally, disruption of our dialogue with God inevitably leads to competition, jealousy, and ultimately to murder of one's brother.

What is learned in subsequent religious history, although implied in Genesis, is that restoration of dialogue with God is impossible without restoration of dialogue with one another.

Becoming our brother's keeper (or friend) is the way of reversing the decision of Adam and Eve. Jesus was the first to do so, preferring to shed his own blood rather than that of his brothers and sisters. Many have since followed his lead. In other words, restoration of dialogue among us will lead us back to the universe as a garden of paradise where we can once again walk with God in dialogue as friends are wont to do.

These three important truths from Genesis are the basic truths underlying SCC: 1) God yearns to be in dialogue with us as a friend, 2) this dialogue necessarily involves our brother and sister (neighbor), and 3) disruption in dialogue leads to violence. God has always been closer to us than we are to ourselves. God's burning desire for heart-to-heart dialogue has never abated. Unfortunately, murder has led to murder so that now the hearts of many have become as hard as stone, shutting out the healing power of loving dialogue. As followers of Jesus we strive to eliminate the poisonous spirit of Cain who has no concern for his brother. The violence and bloodshed that surrounds us is ample evidence that the consequences of our alienation from God have endured.

Importance of Getting Started

You recall that in the introduction we mentioned that reading this book merely to gain a theoretical understanding of SCC will indeed be beneficial to you. However, it will be much more beneficial if you invite one or two friends or neighbors to form SCC with you now so you can start working on restoring dialogue, lost since the time of Adam. As you go through the chapters of this book it is our hope that all of you will grow in both understanding and grace.

Remember the lessons of Genesis: healing of the relationship among us must take place before the healing of friendship with God is possible. Someone must be the initiator, that is, make the deliberate decision to reverse the decision of Adam and Eve. This cannot be done in an abstract reasoning or uninvolved process. So start now with a few other people. If no one comes to mind readily, talk to your pastor or members of your parish council and tell them of your determination to develop SCC. If all else fails, do it the American way and advertise. If you are going to enter the new world paradise through dialogue, for which this book is a guide, you must do it in the company of others.

Sharing Deep Values

Once you have convinced several others to accompany you on your journey, you can begin to experience dialogue in a very real way, not just in theory but in practice. Through dialogue you have the opportunity to learn how to be yourself, leading to an unfolding of your deepest values in the presence of understanding and loving friends. At the same time you provide a similar environment for them. Thus you are approaching SCC as a living reality, not merely as an abstract concept or strategy for social action. As you begin to "find yourself" in greater depth, you will also discover deeper relationships with the friends who accompany you on this journey. Understanding of God, self, and neighbor are inseparably bound up in the Christian vision of life.

The words "in the beginning" set the context not only for your first gathering, but for all gatherings to follow. Each time you come together with friends, it is again a new beginning, because during the intervening time all of you have been exposed to many different events, ideas, and experiences that have changed you. Each gathering, therefore, is fresh, new, and a moment of special grace, never just a routine repetition of a weekly, biweekly, or monthly meeting. It is important that you develop the discipline needed to be constantly aware of this aspect of SCC. Failure to do so will drain your routine meetings of their meaning and potential for growth.

Speaking of regular meetings, you should agree with your friends on a special time to meet on an ongoing basis. This time is to be quality time for all of you, to be changed or disrupted only for serious reasons. Fidelity to a designated time shows that you know how important these meetings are.

Dialogue with Scripture

In preparation for your meetings, each of you should select a Scripture reading that says something to you in your time and place. By sharing the Word of God, you are bringing God into your dialogue. Your effort thereby becomes one of trying to restore the original plan God had with Adam and Eve from the beginning, one in which God and persons were involved in ongoing dialogue and friendship.

When you come together, after you have first had a chance to catch up on the news and concerns you may have, share with one another the Scripture readings you have selected, and discuss their meaning. In so doing you will not only be sharing with friends the values that are important to you but you will also be placing yourselves in an extremely important context. You will be continuing the kind of Christian gatherings that have been used since apostolic times. From the very beginning Christians gathered to share what Christ meant in their daily lives. Do not underestimate the importance of your gathering in this context of historical Christian faith. Your gathering, however small or seemingly insignificant to you, becomes another rivulet that feeds into the mighty stream of believers that have gathered before you in the name of Christ to be transformed, and thereby to transform the face of the earth.

Historical Context

We live in a time when "big" is assumed to be better. Today there is a phenomenal growth of mega-churches in which thousands gather at a time. When it comes to churches, big does not necessarily mean better. Fads come and go. What cannot be stressed enough is that not size but the historical context of your SCC is of great importance. Scripture reading is not to be viewed as just another item on the agenda of your meeting but rather as the means of putting your faith sharing into its proper historical as well as faith context. Where even two come together, a historical context can be preserved.

Thus, the first Christians gathered in homes in small groups for as long as three hundred years after the death of Christ to share the hand-copied letters of apostles and memories of Jesus. It was a long time before their memories of Jesus were actually written in the form of the four gospels. In our television age, it's hard to believe that the gospels are not journalistic snapshots of news events, but rather reflections of the evolving understanding of the first SCCs as they began to sort out the meaning of all the words and deeds of Jesus.

Historically, the gospel accounts came from the early SCCs rather than SCCs from the gospels. Thus, the New Testament tells us more, in a way, about how the first Christians responded to the message of Jesus as they shared among themselves his memories and values then about the historical Jesus himself. Or, put in another way, we understand much more about Jesus by the effect he had on the apostolic SCC whose values and perceptions are reflected in the gospels. Jesus himself wrote nothing that we know of except in the hearts of believers. He continues to do so to this very day. We are fortunate to have Jesus present at our every gathering to guide us. We are also fortunate that people in apostolic times wrote down their memories of Jesus, thus affording us not only a glimpse of Jesus, but a divinely inspired insight into how our SCC can reflect God's beloved son.

These early Christian communities were made up of mainly the poor and women. Women were attracted by the new status of equality accorded them in the teachings of Christianity at a time when women were often little more than slaves. When rich families converted to Christianity, the gatherings became larger because wealthy people lived in large houses able to accommodate larger groups. Eventually, influenced by the Roman emperor Constantine, who confiscated pagan temples and turned them into churches, Christians began to meet in larger gatherings. Consequently, large gatherings become a practice that has endured to our own day. The recent practice of gathering as a SCC is a rediscovery of our ancient roots.

In the World of Today

Your meetings with friends must be viewed not only in terms of biblical times but also in the context of the church of today. Be aware that there are thousands of people in the United States and throughout the world who, like yourselves, come together as SCCs on an ongoing basis to grow in their faith. In South and Central America, especially, the numbers are in the hundreds of thousands.

In the interest of a better understanding of SCC, it is important to note that the environment of SCC in South America is very different from that in the United States and Canada. South American countries have two overpowering social forces that shape culture and, accordingly, spill over into the practice of SCC (called "base communities"). The two powerful forces are a strong sense of tribalism (inherited from their ancient past) and extreme poverty (5 percent of the population owns 90 percent of the wealth). The effects of these two tremendous social forces on SCC are easily predictable. Base communities spread very rapidly because of tribal communication networks already in place (thus accounting for the huge numbers of SCCs there), and the base communities are preoccupied with social justice and liberation of a people crushed by poverty and unjust distribution of money and goods.

In the United States the situation is very different. We have poor people, but not in such huge numbers. Unlike our neighbors to the South we are fortunate to have a large, well educated, middle class. We have numerous welfare programs that provide avenues for the poor to achieve a more satisfying lifestyle. We do not have the atmosphere of hopelessness that characterizes many South American countries. Also, we do not have the strong tribal traditions. Rather, we pride ourselves on being independent, self reliant, and following a make-it-on-your-own philosophy. Furthermore, Americans are aware that the United States has become the envy of the world for the economic progress that is believed to flow from this philosophy of independence and self reliance.

The effects of our culture are very predictable on SCC. Obviously, the spread of small communities will be slow because a tribal syndrome does not prevail, and SCC challenges the tendency to go it alone. Furthermore, most people here are not in dire economic straits. Therefore, SCCs in the United States will not spread as easily.

I am sure the obvious question is forming in your mind: So why launch into the frustrating task of trying to form SCC with a country full of people who are fairly comfortable and who pride themselves on being individualistic and self reliant? First, who said it was going to be easy. Key to the development of SCC in the United States is to avoid any attempt to discard our sense of being an individual and make every effort to build on that notion by seeking a deeper understanding of what being an individual means. This is crucial to the success of SCC in the United States.

Understanding the Individual

Advances in modern psychology are critical to a more perceptive understanding of what being an individual means. Individual does not mean isolated. Individual is better understood as "unique." Each person is not only an individual but at the same time also utterly uniquely individual. Consequently, each of us has a unique relationship with God and, can therefore, reveal a dimension of God that no one else can.

Although we are keenly aware that Jesus is a unique revelation of God, we often fail to realize that each of us, like Jesus, reveals something of God to our world. All of us have received a unique call from God to be who we are and, like Jesus, to reveal the loving God to others through our fidelity to our unique selves.

Advances in modern psychology not only make each of us more aware of our unique individual selves but also explores the meaning of "experiencing" ourselves. Each of us has an experience of the world that no one else has or ever will have because each person constitutes a new synthesis of all of reality. We tend to assume that everyone, or at least those closest to us, have the same experience of life and reality as we do. This is an erroneous assumption.

Psychologists tell us that when we dialogue with another person we are experiencing the other person but we are experiencing ourselves in a way that only happens with that person. Similarly, the other person is experiencing him or herself in a unique way which we alone can evoke, because each of us is also a unique reality.

When we are open to another person, the experience of that person comes into our own self experience like an exquisite melody played on the instrument of my unique identity. By experiencing myself in this new way, I am able to gain a better perception of who I am.

When this happens we have to decide to accept or reject that particular experience of ourselves. Jesus, for example, was experienced by many people and many decisions were consequently made. John the Evangelist delighted in the manifestation of Jesus as the fulfillment of God's promise. Peter wept because he decided to betray Jesus, and Judas hanged himself for a similar reason. Each made a decision as they experienced themselves in the presence of Christ.

Scales fell from his eyes when Saul experienced himself in his own unique relationship with Jesus, and he became the apostle "Paul." This account concerning Paul in Scriptures illustrates that the person of Jesus, even after the tragedy of Calvary, could still evoke a unique experience in each person that is open to him. When Jesus allows us to experience him, we like his first disciples, can choose to accept or reject the experience and in so doing choose who we are to be.

Thus you and your partner in dialogue can experience yourselves as no one else in the world can. You can bring out in one another what no one else can, because both of you are a unique revelation of God. You can enrich one another with new experiences of self and with new awareness.

Individual and Community

If you have never stopped to reflect on these implications of what it means to be an "individual," it's important to do so now because in SCC you are not just a member of a "group" or "tribe," but an individual person with a special identity and gifts. This notion of individual involves both a separate but also a universal element. No one can find fulfillment in isolation from others. Being an individual does not mean, necessarily, that we are in competition. In a SCC we are called, not to compete with one another, but to celebrate one another. In so doing we constantly rediscover ourselves through the unique experience that others evoke in us. Thus we will form a new understanding of self, God and neighbor. To put this in another way: a true friend not only allows us to be ourselves (that is, experience ourselves) but adds new color to the experience by serving as a mirror to reflect a dimension of self that we have never before seen.

You may want to read and reread these last few paragraphs until it becomes clear to you that "individual" and "community" are not mutually exclusive concepts. Many of us have been raised with great emphasis on conformity for the common good, very much as members of a tribe are forced into conformity through laws and regulations for the good of the whole tribe. The idea of a whole society based on individual rights, such as we have in the United States, is somewhat new in world history. Generally, nations are based on tribal structures. You may go to Italy but you can never become Italian. You can come to America and become American overnight because your citizenship is based upon being an individual, not on being a member of a particular tribe. When you stop and reflect on what experiencing yourself as an individual means as explained above, it will seem like belaboring the obvious. But nothing is closer to us than our own self experience and therefore is painfully hard to analyze. It is like trying to see your own face without the aid of a mirror.

It is necessary to reflect on these "mechanics" of self experience because they are important in entering into SCC. SCC means a coming together of individuals through dialogue, rather than a coming together of members of a group to engage in some spiritual, academic or social enterprise. By entering into SCC you do not, however, and should not lose your individuality. To the contrary, if it is truly a community (contrasted with a "tribe" in which no one has a unique identity except the tribal chief), your individuality will become the very source of life through which the community can grow. SCC thereby reflects the central mystery of Christianity, namely, the Blessed Trinity in which is found the uniqueness of persons, oneness in being and equality in majesty.

Dialogue and the Individual

This brings us back again to what is both the beginning and end of SCC, namely, dialogue. Only in dialogue can we become the unique persons we are called to be. SCC is not just a group or an organization but an "event" in which those who come together receive the grace of one another. In other words, each person's self is re-created by the unique self of the other persons in the gathering. It is a grace because in the process the God who is calling each of us is being more fully revealed as each becomes more him or herself through dialogue. This ongoing process is the very source of life for SCC.

At this point let's take a further look at the meaning of dialogue. When we are in dialogue, we speak from the heart and in so doing and at the same time we are learning to listen from the heart. To put it in another way, if we cannot speak from the heart we cannot hear the heart of another speaking. When we speak from what is truly in our hearts rather than from political, manipulative, or prejudicial assumptions, we are creating an atmosphere for another person to also speak and ultimately listen from the heart. When this occurs, both are changed forever because a new world is unfolding in the process, a world in which the God of love becomes more visible.

When we speak from the heart, there is a sense of joy that accompanies the growing process. But in so doing, we become vulnerable and may experience pain due to ridicule, rejection, or misunderstanding. Dialogue does not come easily but is the result of patience and the hard work of being true to oneself and allowing others to do likewise.

Dialogue with others cannot be separated from the divine-human dialogue in our hearts. Communion with God and neighbor is basic to Christian belief. How can we love God whom we cannot see if we do not love our neighbor whom we do see? (1 John 4:20). We cannot separate communion with God and neighbor. For John, and for Jesus, they formed the two sides of the same coin. Therefore, whenever we come together in loving dialogue, we are loving God whom we cannot see.

Conclusion

Thus far, we have defined the "context" of SCC, the importance of which cannot be stressed enough. Context is analogous to where a tree is planted. If planted in a small container, the tree will be miniature in size. If planted in a larger container to perhaps adorn a shopping mall, the tree can grow to a much larger size. But, if planted in the rich soil of open spaces, the tree can grow to fill the sky with its branches. So, too, the coming together of you and your SCC partner must constantly be placed in a context that will expand your lives to someday encompass the whole of humanity and the God who beckons us all.

So, you have made a beginning. Gathering with others to share Scripture, to read and discuss this book in the context of your daily lives, and to share your life stories, you are able to grow in love and appreciation of one another. In your efforts to form a SCC, you have moved your relationships into a new context. This new context has tremendously important implications. The dialogue (relationships) that you have achieved must become inclusive, not exclusive. To pursue SCC you must now extend your dialogue to include others. In doing so the level of dialogue within your SCC will not be diluted but deepened.

The next chapter will focus on steps to develop inclusive love. Before beginning the next chapter, however, you might try to expand your group to six to ten people. As mentioned previously, it is much easier to understand the material presented in the next chapters if you are going through the experiences being discussed with at least ten people.

A Final Caution

At this point an important caution should be brought to your attention and that is: Don't be in a hurry. SCC is a growth process, a way of life, not a task to be started and done with. The mark of the survivor in SCC is patience. You may wish to continue meeting with your original small group for a number of months or even a year before moving on to the next chapter. If you rush to develop SCC without placing it in the right context it will not survive any more than a fish could out of water. God has been working from the beginning to restore dialogue with humankind. Your SCC needs to bring this cosmic struggle into focus. You do not work alone but can take your place among thousands before you who have struggle to restore the harmony of paradise.

As you meet to share your thoughts about the context of SCC and to explore the gospels, you will no doubt have many questions about beginning SCC. The questions and answers that follow may be helpful in stimulating a discussion in your own SCC. These are followed by discussion questions aimed at reviewing the content of this chapter.

QUESTIONS AND ANSWERS

Q. I find it easy to get together with someone else to talk about faith and values. How can this be viewed as a religious activity, and how can it be the start of a small Christian community?

A. The enjoyment you share is at the heart of the Christian experience. In the pursuit of meaningful relationships, however, you will also sometimes encounter painful obstacles not unlike those Christ encountered when he pursued a relationship with his friends. Since person-to-person relationship is the basis of all relationships, even a gathering of two in the name of Christ merits the designation of SCC.

Q. In our gatherings we discuss recent events and read meaningful Scripture selections, but then we run out of material and seem to be wasting time. What can we do to be more productive?

A. Remember that developing a small faith community is more a matter of growing or becoming, than it is a matter of doing. We North Americans tend to be preoccupied with goals, objectives, organization, evaluation and production. SCC, however, is a creation of grace and can't be mass produced. That said, we suggest that you use the first chapter of this book for your upcoming gatherings. It will offer you a context in which to come together based on true dialogue. It will guide your discussions about the meaning of dialogue, the importance of being individuals, and the significance of discovering who you are in dialogue.

Q. How long should we take before we move on to the second chapter?

A. All that follows in this book will be, in essence, an expansion of the dialogue that you have begun with your small group. As the dialogue grows, you will appreciate more and more the context of your relationship as spelled out in this first chapter. The decision to move on should be a mutual decision based on your feelings of readiness to delve more deeply into the demands of dialogue.

Q. I'm not sure what it means to "experience" myself through dialogue. Can you elaborate on this?

A. In the Western world we think of ourselves in external or functional terms such as father/mother, electrician, secretary, plumber, black/white, male/female, rich/poor, young/old, and the like. As you know, Christianity has Eastern origins and, in keeping with Eastern cultures, assumes that "experience" is far more important than external characteristics or functions. This is why Paul made the comment that when a person comes to faith there is "neither Jew or Gentile, slave or free, male or female, for all are anointed of God" (Galatians 3:28). Paul is referring to an experience that goes to the very core of an individual. Who you are is much more important than what you have acquired. Granted, it's very hard for us to focus on an experience of ourselves that is more fundamental than what we do.

As you develop a small community, however, it will become more apparent to you that community is not a "thing," but the result of a living and dynamic dialogue between individuals who are becoming aware of who they are and who are learning more about their call each time they gather in the name of Christ.

Q. Why do you use the words "coming together" when you refer to meeting with a few friends? Is there a special significance to these words?

A. Indeed there is a special significance to the words "coming together." The Christian notion of sin is deceit, disruption, division, disharmony and all that breed violence, hatred, ambition, greed, and many other ills. When we say "coming together" we mean to reflect the healing grace of God that counters the cancer of sin. "Coming together" refers above all to the struggle of restoring harmony in our own hearts. As this occurs, we share life-giving peace with others, with family members, friends, neighbors, and the world community until it envelops all of Earth. This is the same peace that Christ felt and passed on to us.

Q. Is the context of our meeting more important than what goes on at the meeting?

A. Context is all important. What goes on at SCC has as its sole purpose to put us into the proper context. The ultimate context a follower of Christ must achieve is to live as the beloved of God. We help each other achieve this by creating a SCC in which this reality becomes visible. That is, if we treat each other for who we are by divine calling, then it becomes much easier for each of us to become conscious of who we are.

Q. We have been meeting for some time now and some complain of boredom. What should I do?

A. It could be a sign that you are ready for the challenges of chapter two and maybe should move on. However, remember that doing exercises to stay physically fit are often boring, but we must do them or suffer health problems. We live in a time when family and community life is breaking down. We can no longer take relationships for granted, but must make a conscious effort to pursue meaningful dialogue with others. Your group's "community"" muscles may be so out of shape that it is painful to get them moving again. In that case, the only response to boredom is discipline which underlies all real progress.

Q. Since there are so many different translations of the Bible, which one should we use for our Scripture reflections?

A. In large groups, where conformity is critical to reaching a common goal, this issue is very important. In small groups, however, where dialogue between persons is critical, the issue of which Bible to use should be an individual and not a group choice. The Bible selected should represent an effort on the part of each individual to share personal understanding of God's Word. This sharing should be exchanged with respect and reverence. For the vitality of a small faith community, it is very important that members speak from the heart. So each of you should choose a translation that you are comfortable with. It's not necessary to read along from a common text. What is important is that the Word of God be heard and shared.

Q. My friends and I have discussed at great length whether members of SCC should focus on themselves as individual persons or on building up "community." What do you think?

A. You might recall that central to the Judeo-Christian tradition is the notion that God is in dialogue with people. Jesus is the word (dialogue) of God made flesh. Dialogue is, by definition, between two persons and only secondarily involves the community. Community in effect is the overflow of person-to-person dialogue.

Community, therefore, is secondary, an effect, not a cause. Jesus has invited us as his disciples to enter into dialogue with the Father through the Holy Spirit, who will remind us of all that Jesus has said and done. As a consequence of our reflection on Christ's words and deeds, we will be able to do works far greater than Jesus has done (John 14:12). This person-to-person dialogue is the ultimate source of all power in the church, a process reaching a fullness in Jesus who is the Word of God. It will continue until all his disciples are in communion with the Father. This event will constitute the end of time because when love is complete time flies.

Q. Discussion in our small community sometimes strays from religion into politics and other contemporary issues and arguments are often the result. Are we on the wrong track?

A. Without knowing more about your group, it seems that you are. The underlying reason a small community of faith gathers is to focus on faith topics and Scripture, recognizing that each person is a unique gift of God's love to the whole group. Members of a small group should occasionally feel free to dialogue on any subject, but if your gatherings are becoming political debates, you have probably carried this principle too far. Save the political debates for your social time afterwards.

Q. My friends and I have known one another for years. What would gathering as SCC add?

A. Getting to know someone is only the first step toward a community experience that ultimately leads to communion with God and neighbor. Furthermore, getting to know other people progresses through many stages from the most superficial to the deepest levels of communication. The Scripture story about Martha and Mary is a good example of this. Martha knew Jesus at the social level of sharing a meal with him; Mary, her sister, knew him at a deeper level of sharing the word of life with him.

No matter how well you know people there is always more to know and appreciate. Sharing personal insights about Scripture will stimulate the process of revelation. In this same process people come to a greater knowledge and understanding of themselves. So you see, knowing people as friends is one thing; knowing them in the search for deeper faith is quite another.

Q. I am confused! I have heard people refer to SCC as a group, circle, meeting, church, discussion club, assembly, and who knows what else. Can you put a label on this development in the church?

A. This issue is an excellent topic for discussion in a small gathering as a way of defining what it is that the gathering is all about. The sensitivity of each person obviously needs to be considered in arriving at a label. It is of much greater importance that the gathering, whatever it is called, create an environment for members to grow as persons of faith and love.

It is worthy of note that the word "group" emphasizes organization and action, for example, dividing into groups to attain an objective. "Circle" and "club" generally emphasize discussion and social activity. "Church" derives from the Greek word for "assembly" and signifies simply a "calling together." When people respond to the call, that is when they form "church," it is then possible to pray, worship, discuss, plan social action, or simply grow as persons of faith as a result of the coming together. Each gathering, however small, can be viewed as a microcosm of the universal call of all humankind. But each group needs to determine its own identity.

Q. I know that Christ is present in the tabernacle, but how is he present in a gathering of a small community such as ours?

A. The basic issue is not how? but why? Christ is present in the tabernacle or small community of faith. Once you understand the why, the how will be obvious.

The reason Christ is present in the tabernacle is to engage us in a heart-to-heart dialogue when we walk into the church, much like we would expect to dialogue with any friends when we walk into their homes. Thus, the why of Christ's presence in the tabernacle is to foster this heartfelt dialogue.

When we walk into a small gathering called together by the love of Christ, the dialogue with Christ going on in the hearts of all present is shared in the course of the meeting. The same dialogue Christ initiates in our hearts when we sit or kneel in front of a tabernacle, he initiates in the hearts of our friends by attracting them to a meeting and sparking with his Spirit the dialogue of sharing among all participants. The big difference is, in a small community the dialogue is audible. When a loving dialogue reaches the same level of unreserved self-giving love that Christ achieved in the process of dialoguing with his small community of friends, then and only then, we will know Christ in his risen fullness. In due time, the why of his presence will give way to how he is present in history, namely, as the bond of love uniting all humankind.

QUESTIONS FOR REVIEW AND DISCUSSION

1. What is dialogue and how does it differ from a discussion, a lecture, a conversation, and a monologue?

2. What is meant by the "context" of a situation? Give examples. Why is it an important issue in understanding SCC?

3. How is Christ present in SCC?

4. Has your relationship changed any since you began developing SCC?

5. What does it mean to be an individual? Why is it important in SCC to have a deeper understanding of SCC?

6. What do you mean by "faith" in the context of "individual"?

7. Women especially were attracted to the first SCCs. Why? Is that true today? Why?

8. How do SCCs in North America differ from those in South America? What can we learn from the difference?

9. Why is patience the bedrock of SCC? How can a person achieve patience?

10. Why are "individual" and "community" two sides of the same coin? Can one exist without the other? Explain.

Chapter 2

The Upper Room

Shortly before Jesus died, he gathered with his twelve disciples, prayed intensely that they would become as one, and gave his body and blood to bring about the communion that he sought promising to be with them to the end of time. Soon after Jesus was crucified, the disciples, in mortal fear and total confusion, again gathered in the upper room to begin sorting out the meaning of all that had transpired from the day they were first called by Jesus, to the sad event of Calvary, to the startling news of the empty tomb. The disciples pondered the implications of all that Jesus said and did for each of them individually as well as for the community of disciples as a whole.

Like the first disciples, a small Christian community (SCC) is called to ponder the significance of Jesus for each individual

vidual as well as for the members as a whole. The fear and confusion that characterized the small group of disciples in the upper room are present today in every SCC confronted with the violence, change, and complexity of our modern world. Like the earliest disciples, SCC members reflect in their hearts and enter into dialogue with friends who, like themselves, are called together to bring the risen Christ once again into our world.

In Chapter 1, we focused on Christian dialogue between two or more friends. In the interest of further growth, the dialogue that began with two or three people should now be expanded to include a larger number, if possible, eight to ten people. Let people know of your goal to form SCC, and you will probably be surprised to discover how ready many are for something more in spiritual development.

Some people may object that they are already too busy and have neither the time nor the energy to join SCC. Point out to them that SCC does not drain energy but refreshes its members, making it possible to make better use of time that is thought to be in short supply. Above all, be patient in pursuing your goal of creating SCC as there is intense competition in the world for the minds and hearts of people. Many are naturally suspicious of anything new. SCC may sound just too good to be true.

More Complex Dialogue

At the first meeting of new members interested in developing SCC, it would be inappropriate to outline a step-by-step agenda that would guarantee success. All members are embarking on a voyage in the trackless sea of life. The SCC itself must make the decisions regarding what it will do and what it will become. In this chapter we will try to point out issues and cautions that will help all of you see what SCC looks like from the inside. Once you have gained an understanding, you will be able to explore the new world on your own.

As you progress in your efforts to come together as an expanded SCC, it will become very obvious that the process of entering into dialogue with one another is dramatically more complex. From the start you should be conscious that creating dialogue in a community with eight to ten members is a colossal task. Look upon the endeavor as a monumental work of art surpassing the finest cathedral ever built. In reality, what you endeavor to do is more lasting than stone and mortar. Creating SCC touches upon the very core of life itself because we are seeking to enter into communion (dialogue) with one another using as model, inspiration, and cause the communion that exists from all eternity between the divine persons in the Holy Trinity. This life of communion within the Trinity to which we are invited was first made visible in Jesus and is now being made manifest in all who follow after him.

As you begin anew understand well that the original dialogue between two or three that has led to a communion of lives, will not become diluted because of the inclusion of others, but rather greatly deepened and enriched. The dialogue developed in the small group will in time influence other members and assist all to seek a quality of union that will increasingly reflect the depth set for us by Jesus who freely laid down his life on our behalf.

Who Should Lead?

As your SCC pursues its life of dialogue, leadership is the first issue that needs clarification. In SCC, leadership demands the skills of a tight rope walker. The group as a whole must be seen as exercising leadership but at the same time the initiative of leadership rests with every member. For a successful SCC, each member must become the world's greatest initiator and follower. It takes experience and great wisdom to know which to pursue at a given time. Strange as it may seem, the most effective leader in SCC knows when to be the most enthusiastic follower of another's initiative.

Christian leadership is not to be perceived as economic or militaristic in style. Rather, it consists in a keen awareness of the nature of influence and mastery of the ability to direct influence to bring about communion within oneself and, as a consequence, into one's environment. Jesus constantly drew crowds to himself and then frequently admonished those drawn by his influence to do as he has done in order to draw others.

The gospels capture the words and deeds of Christ so that his influence not only endures to the present day and for all ages to come but also so that we can learn the new type of leadership Jesus introduces to the world. Perhaps the best example in our own day of this new type of leadership is Pope John XXIII. He exercised a remarkable influence on the whole world, both personally and through the Vatican Council he summoned.

Though your SCC may not be a coming together on the grand scale of a world council, it is no less important. When you gather, you are constantly influencing others in positive or negative ways. The more you place your gathering in the context of the gospels, the more you are replacing negative influences with life giving influence that flow from the gospels, from Christ, and ultimately from God.

To achieve this you sometimes have to work through hurt feelings, jealousy, envy, wounded pride, disappointment, and a host of other afflictions that can threaten dialogue. But this give and take can also lead to an exciting new world in which one can walk with others feeling no need to dominate or be subjugated. This new kind of leadership yields a oneness based upon an equality of persons that is a foretaste of our life of communion with Christ and all who respond to him.

To put the matter in practical terms: it is most appropriate for the person who began your SCC to have taken the initiative to call the community together. This person must now have the humility to become the follower as the group begins to

SCC. The small community now, as a whole, must decide what it wishes to become. This does not preclude individual initiative in defining what the gathering is about. In so doing the individual is revealing what he or she is about and sets the stage for dialogue and growth.

The exercise as well as the development of leadership is the primary reason for keeping the gathering small. Some people have the tendency to take over while others tend to sit back and just go along. It is unfair to oneself as well as to others to consistently take a dominating role of leadership or a passive role of follower. If the gathering becomes too large (15 or more) these two very human tendencies take over and dialogue becomes the first casualty. Dissolution of the SCC may soon follow. As a rule of thumb, the smaller the gathering, the easier it is to create an atmosphere of dialogue. In a smaller gathering, domineering or laid back behavior become more obvious thus making corrective action much more likely through the healing powers of Christ.

Thriving on Diversity

The unique beauty of each person has opportunity to blossom if the community remains small so that the interaction of personality types becomes a refining rather than an irritating process. A random gathering of people in SCC will certainly represent a rainbow of personalities. These personalities range from the competitive, hard-driving, impatient, anger-prone workaholic racing toward a heart attack to the laid back, uninvolved dreamer floating in the clouds.

Chances are that members of your gathering do not match either an aggressive or passive prototype, however. Everyone falls somewhere in between. It should be noted that we need both the driver and the dreamer, the crusader and the contemplative, the speaker and the listener. For SCC to prosper, the personality types of the members must be balanced against each other to insure a pursuit of practical action as well as

Christian ideals. Only continued meeting and humble patience will bring about the polishing needed on each personality so the deeper unique beauty of each person is brought out.

Perhaps an even greater threat to achieving our goal of person-to-person dialogue is the diverse occupations of the members of SCC. Diversity caused by occupation are derived from various professional, economic, or political activities in which a member is involved. Religious and ethnic background may add even more complexity. It is especially difficult for Americans who tend to think of their identity in terms of the social position achieved through their job, the make of the car they drive, the religion they practice, or their ethnic background. In a large gathering, these distinctions may serve a purpose, but status due to background is of small consequence in SCC compared to the dignity and value of each person.

A well educated doctor, judge, or lawyer will undoubtedly find it very difficult to relate to a factory worker, a cleaning lady, or store clerk on the equal basis required for person-to-person dialogue. It may be helpful to remember that whatever gifts we possess are for the sake of the community, even as God shares with us beyond measure. Infinitely more important than the gift, social status, acquired possessions, or mastery of skills is the dignity of the underlying person in whom the human-divine dialogue comes into focus in our time and place. Amplification of this human-divine dialogue within the heart of each person, regardless of the person's social standing, for the direction and edification of the whole community is the sole purpose of your SCC.

Differences in racial or religious background can become especially difficult barriers to dialogue, if care is not taken. In large gatherings, religion and race historically have led to division. In a small gathering it is possible to deal more effectively with divisive issues because the person underlying the race or religious belief is more visible, and therefore more likely to evoke the healing love needed for delving into a dialogue on divisive elements. When confrontation is needed, the accepting atmosphere of SCC is able to quickly soothe and heal hurt feelings thus making it possible for the SCC to survive and grow in truth and in love.

Need for Strategies

As mentioned previously, it is inappropriate to lay out in advance a step-by-step agenda for building SCC because the evolving life of your SCC will reflect the individual persons involved. An atmosphere must be created in which both the small community as a whole can make decisions and at the same time leadership initiative can come from individual members. Give and take in the process of moving forward toward the ideals Christ has set for his disciples creates the dialogue that is the heartbeat of SCC.

Every SCC with more than two or three members, however, needs strategies that serve to establish a framework for dialogue to occur. These strategies should be understood by all in the gathering and then formal planning must take place to utilize those strategies in a way that best serve the particular needs of each SCC.

The first strategy for building community is to provide time for greeting one another. This fits in naturally upon arriving where the gathering is to take place. Obviously, the initial greeting cannot be programmed. The greeting, however, must be real, that is, it must express what the members truly feel toward one another. The world is filled with pretense and manipulation. SCC is attractive because it is an oasis where persons can be refreshed by touching what is genuine. Each member, in striving to be genuine, creates an influence inviting others to be likewise. From the very first encounter Christian leadership is thus being exercised.

The strategy of greeting should extend into the first part of a meeting because members have been separated for a period of time during which many things have happened. In reality you have become strangers to one another due to the intervening influences since the last meeting. Regardless of how many meetings have taken place previously, the present meeting is always approached as the first at which members need to be reacquainted. We must guard against stereotyping each other but rather be always cognizant that intervening personal experiences can bring about subtle and sometimes profound changes in a person since the last time the SCC met.

A greeting strategy for the first part of a meeting consists of allowing time for each member to bring up whatever has occurred since the last meeting. It may be something personal, something related to family or friends, or a pressing political or religious issue important to the member. Whatever each member feels important ought to be shared and freely discussed with the other members. This initial process serves to acknowledge the importance of each member, highlights change as a reality of life, provides an opportunity for the healing power of the SCC to occur as needed, and allows people to clear away what may be preoccupying them so that there can be more responsiveness to what will happen as the gathering together progresses.

Readings to Foster Dialogue

Another strategy for dialogue, not necessarily the second step in the process of a gathering, is to provide time for discussion of a serious article or part of a book. SCC should agree on what should be read and discussed for the educational enrichment of all the members. Members should have a copy of the material to be discussed before the meeting so that each has had time to reflect on the issues raised. This strategy will foster a greater understanding of the Christian way of life, help members put on the mind of Christ, and provide a deeper understanding of the values that each member holds.

An indispensable strategy that should be used to bring the gathering to a deeper level of dialogue is the reading of sacred

Scripture and sharing of what it means in one's own life of faith and its meaning for the SCC as a whole. Like the founding fathers of our country who wrote a constitution for the United States to preserve justice and freedom for all, so too the first Christians wrote the Scriptures as a constitution to ensure the authenticity of the Christian community to the end of time. Every Christian community must delve into the Scriptures to constantly rediscover what it means to be under the influence (kingdom) of God, just as all laws and judgments in our country must be scrutinized in the light of the constitution established by our founding fathers.

The Scriptures, however, in one important aspect, are unlike any human document. The Constitution of the United States is the supreme law to which all must conform. The Scriptures are not in the form of a rigid law to which all must conform but the foot steps of a people who have found God. Words in the Scriptures are like foot steps in the sand beckoning us to follow.

The Scriptures are meant to serve as guideposts as each person struggles in his or her heart to enter into dialogue with God. The Scriptures serve their purpose if they accomplish this. One, therefore, need not be a Scripture scholar to read the sacred texts. What is important is what the Scripture passage is saying to the individual for whom it was intended. It is important not only to the spiritual development of the individual but also to the growth of the SCC in which the meaning of the Scriptures is being shared.

The Scriptures are intended to open, rather than program, our hearts. In so doing we release the influence of God embodied in the sacred text. It is ironic that the whole world today is rushing toward the democracy embodied in the American Constitution while the good news embodied in the divine constitution of the gospel seems to fall on deaf ears. Could it be that the Christian community that ought to embody the influence of a loving God recorded in the Scriptures is no where to be seen?

Both Old and New Testaments should be used. For thousands of years, from the time of Abraham, our ancestors in faith, to the advent of Christ, believers have struggled to conceptualize God. In ancient times, God was seen as identical with life itself, that is, a living force behind all nature. In the days of Moses, God drew much closer because Moses introduced the image of God as chieftain of the tribe of Israel. For the first time, God enters human history as an active participant. The Old Testament records the words and actions of God as divine chief of the chosen people as well as the evolution of that image of God by the people of Israel.

Understanding the Old Testament prepares the believer to make a quantum leap to an espousal God, introduced by Christ, as the ultimate image of God. Perception of God in an espousal relationship with each person is the basic theology underlying SCC. Large groups naturally turn to a tribal image of God as leader or father in order to function effectively. Large national churches today still make use of the image of God as supreme lord or master. Devotees submit to the will of these churches as a way of submitting to the will of God, perceived as the divine leader. This image makes little sense in SCC, where relationship is person to person, not follower to leader. One must, however, develop in his or her faith life through the God imaging of the Old Testament before one is ready to make the leap of faith reflected in the New Testament in which we come face to face (that is, enter into direct dialogue) with God. The dialogue we pursue with each other is the path that tunes us into the dialogue with God that is the very core of our being.

We will come back to the importance of our imaging of God in future chapters. Our focus here is on reading of Scripture as a strategy for dialogue. We can trace the progression of human-divine dialogue through the Old Testament to its fullness in the New. Each of us must make the same journey of faith. That is why Scripture reading is so indispensable in SCC.

Along with what we learn in the Scriptures, the image of God that members of SCC hold to be central to their spiritual life is important to be shared so that other SCC members can clarify their own image of God. This sharing of personal faith is done in the context of Scriptures that records the progress of humankind's journey through the vital, tribal, an espousal imaging of God so that all can discern the path laid out for us in the Bible and gauge their own progress in understanding.

Bringing God into the Dialogue

This brings us to the next strategy for dialogue that may be utilized by your SCC and that is one of shared prayer. The apostles listened to Christ for months, then, as an obvious conclusion of what they had heard, asked him to teach them how to pray. Jesus replied that when we pray we should address God as "Our Father...." In other words, the prayers to God that are most authentic and touch upon our deepest longings have the effect of not only uniting one to God, but at the same time to one another. We do not have a God that isolates but one who draws us into communion with one another thereby becoming not "my" Father, but "our" Father.

Many have been raised in a tradition of private prayer and devotion in which only God and oneself are in the picture. Many receive holy communion at Mass and then bury their faces in their hands to be in a world alone with God. Religion for many has become a very personal matter, something that is no one else's business. Expressing prayer as both a personal and communal need requires a giant step in spiritual development.

The easiest way to introduce shared prayer is to connect it with the reading and discussion of sacred Scripture. The spirit of prayer runs throughout the Scriptures, especially the New Testament. Remember that the gospels are the shared memories of the first SCC that met to pray and preserve the words and deeds of Jesus.

Prayer should not be forced but allowed to grow as the

SCC develops. In prayer each member is coming to grips with who he or she is, namely, the beloved of God. That cannot be rushed. Likewise, through the process of prayer, the gathering itself is evolving with a consciousness of its identity as the continuation of Christ throughout history in a particular time and place.

Socializing Extends Dialogue

Another important strategy that the gathering can use in planning for its development is that of socializing. The most obvious activity that promotes socializing is to share in a meal or refreshments. Furthermore, coming together in one hope and one love is to be seen commencing not just at the time the meeting begins. Preparations for a tasty meal to share together, getting into a car and driving to the meeting, eating the food during the gathering and cleaning up after, are all involved in the "coming together."

Doing mundane things such as driving a car or preparing a dish are as important as reading Scripture or sharing prayer in the process of coming together. Do not departmentalize your life. All that you are and do by way of the love and concern shown to one another manifest God's saving grace. Whatever one does derives its importance and value from the dignity of the one acting, that dignity being the beloved of God. Obviously, therefore, a strategy of socializing is very important in the life of SCC since it helps members to see their life of faith in a wider context.

Planning Needed to Foster Dialogue

As mentioned at the beginning of this chapter, since dialogue in a gathering of 10 to 12 is far more difficult and complex than it is between just two persons, a strategy of planning needs to be a part of the process. Planning takes in such obvious concerns as when and where to meet, how often and how long will the meeting be. What mix of strategies to foster dialogue should be used? Who will prepare and lead future meetings? What educational materials and Scripture readings should be utilized?

Planning also includes the more difficult task of identifying more distant goals to be achieved by your SCC as well as the concrete objectives to be attained on the way toward the desired goal. The struggle to envision a worthy goal for your community, together with specific objectives, is a strategy to insure a sense of progress thus guarding against aimless drifting.

The ultimate goal of SCC is consciousness of one's call as the beloved of God that at the same time leads to communion with God and one another. This goal, however, is far too difficult for us to grasp and therefore must be broken down into sub goals that are attainable. This is done through planning. Because planning is an exhausting exercise it is highly recommended that your SCC make a concerted effort to focus exclusively on evaluation and planning during one session each year.

A Time of Special Grace

When the gathering is coming to a close, a final effort to develop dialogue can be accomplished through the use of a strategy for departure. This strategy, like the greeting strategy, is of great importance because it serves to crystalize a sense of mission and reemphasize the dignity of each person. We must be constantly aware that each individual is in the process of being transformed through the influence of faith and love experienced in the SCC so that each is enabled to recognize his or herself as the beloved of God. This transforming grace will radiate to others who are encountered as a member resumes his or her daily life.

The departure strategy should focus to a large extent on expressing appreciation to each other for the person's willingness to be at the SCC meeting. One of the greatest services we can render one another is to come and be with each other. This is the one great service God has rendered to us: God is Emmanuel, always with us. Our efforts to appreciate others who are willing to come and be with us is the means by which we can grow to understand what God being with us means.

The departure strategy is for the most part a spontaneous event needing little actual planning. Even though it seems natural and unplanned, the departure must serve as a grace to make each member aware that a new dimension of dialogue is beginning. Even though members are separate from one another, they remain in communion. Presence to one another is not restricted to physical presence. For unbelievers, out of sight means out of mind. This is not the case with members of SCC. The dialogue at the time of departure should be leading us to a resolve for a greater quality of presence to one another that time and space do not diminish. Thus, members will grow in ever greater appreciation for one another.

SCC may employ only one strategy to foster dialogue, for example, a strategy of prayer or Scripture reading and discussion. One or all strategies may be used according to the need and desires of each SCC. The strategies have no value in and of themselves but serve only as tools to bring about dialogue which is the source of life for the SCC as well as for each member. We should be aware of how to foster dialogue within our community, but we should also be alert to behaviors that disrupt or block the free flow of heart-felt dialogue. Difficulties experienced can be times of special grace and opportunities for growth.

Hostility in SCC

Perhaps the most frequent obstacle to dialogue is that of hostility, for whatever reason, leading to conflict between members. Psychologists tell us that hostility is not a cure for hostility. There is no quick and easy solution to resolve the antagonism one or more members of a small community may have. Other members of the SCC must be willing to suffer through the sorting out process needed when conflict arises. A response of patient and healing love will, in due time, bring the offending member to the realization that the turmoil is within his or her own heart. The afflicted member may gradually recognize that there is something in him or herself that is painful to face and hostility is selected as a way of escape. Or the member may come to realize that he or she is unwilling to let other members be themselves.

Members strive to sort out their identity, many things are going to be said, not out of conviction but as a process of defining where people are in their search for truth and deeper values. No one should be offended by what another says because in a dialogue situation each is allowed freely to sort out his or her values in the presence of people who love them as the beloved of God.

The best practical way to handle conflict in SCC is to use questions, not answers, in responding to those involved in the passion related to hostility. Answers in the form of statements tend to invite reaction from an angry person rather than response. If members, in a healing way, ask meaningful questions, it will help the persons involved in conflict to begin sorting out where the misunderstandings or misconceptions are. Questions imply the humility needed to be a listener. If your SCC is to survive and grow, there must be a great deal of humility and patience among the members. Remember also that the whole idea of being a small community is so that conflict can be healed at a personal level and not overflow into violence which is often the case in large groups or in society at large.

Indifference in SCC

The opposite of anger and conflict is passivity or indifference. If the SCC finds it difficult to redirect hostility to something constructive, drawing life from an attitude of indifference will be found to be far more challenging. An attitude of indifference may be covering any of a multitude of other problems. The passivity may be a form of stress burnout, disillusionment, agnostic rejection of anything spiritual, a guise for superiority, a long repressed anger, or a host of other possibilities including potentially serious health problems that sap energy.

SCC may be able to survive with one or two members that display a noticeable level of indifference, but if the number becomes larger, the SCC will suffer because of the dead weight and may not survive. The root of indifference is a denial of the calling to be the beloved of God. Other members of the SCC, who are trying to respond to an espousal relationship with God, need to express kindness and love by word and deed to a member paralyzed by indifference. We do not know how long members will be required to administer the healing sacrament of their personal love and concern before the icy indifference of a member begins to melt. God alone, who sees the heart, knows when the efforts of SCC will bear fruit in the form of loving response and initiative.

Perhaps the greatest caution of all is to guard against judging an individual. When another causes us pain there is a strong tendency to judge and even condemn the other person. Remember each time you become consciously a healing sacrament of love to another who causes pain by not responding, you will be experiencing love as God experiences it, namely as the initiator. If you do this habitually you will grow in your understanding of God who initiates a loving dialogue with us through all of creation from the beginning of time. This is the only sure path to truly understand God and find the peace and freedom that goes with understanding.

It is worthy of note here that accepting another person with all that person's limitations based on the truth that God does the same is the basic theology underlying the sacrament of penance. In the apostolic Christian communities the love a member experienced enabled the person to see his or her limitations and face these personal failures with faith and courage knowing that the SCC had already forgiven personal faults even before a deficiency was acknowledged by the offender. By medieval times, SCC had faded from memory, having been replaced by large church buildings and worship in sizeable crowds. Christian believers no longer saw their failures as obstacles for entering into the deeper dialogue that constituted the life of SCC, but as violations of church laws. They then began confessing their sins to the parish priest who was now looked upon as representative of the whole community. Instead of being reconciled with the community, the offender sought reconciliation from the priest. A person could no longer feel the forgiveness SCC could extend even before the offender was aware of his or her failing toward the community. The net result is that the concept of church drifted more and more toward a legalistic entity that persists to our own day.

Absenteeism in SCC

Another obstacle to growth in a life of loving dialogue is absenteeism. Any member that will be missing a gathering should at least notify the host family. The one who suffers most is the one who misses the meeting. It is impossible to convey in words what transpires at a gathering. When we come together in the name of Christ, there are special graces received at the time that cannot be captured in words. Even so, every effort should be made to contact the missing member(s) to share what transpired at the meeting.

The SCC is hurt when a member is absent, but here again, a negative can be turned into a positive by members investing even more of themselves. In this situation, members should take note of how often the dialogue becomes deeper with fewer members. This experience should serve to highlight the need for concerted effort to draw everyone out when the whole community is present and when conversation tends to float on the surface. Dialogue is an achievement, and the smaller the gathering the easier it is. However, our ability to dialogue should grow in depth as well as in breadth. The larger the gathering, the greater the challenge.

As a rule, the day(s) of the month selected for the routine gathering of your SCC should not be changed to accommodate members who must be absent. The time for your gathering is a sacred time because the event will be a source of grace that will deeply touch the lives of all participants. The religious practice of gathering in the name of Christ is the great event of our life and therefore must not be seen as something to be displaced with other concerns or activities however important for the moment. From a practical viewpoint, having a set time for gathering, however often, fosters a habit conducive to making the gathering an integral part of one's life. Members will find it easier to arrange their schedules if the day of the gathering has become fixed in their minds and on their calendars.

Having a firmly fixed time for SCC to meet does not mean that SCC cannot change the frequency of meeting. Whatever change is made, however, must be viewed with a sense of permanency so as not to give the impression of "fitting in" the meeting along with our other busy activities. Coming together to enter into dialogue with one another as a path to entering dialogue with God is not just another activity but constitutes a way of life and therefore must be treated with a dignity that such a sacred encounter deserves.

This does not mean that every member must be at every meeting. Obviously, there are many personal reasons that can make it impossible to attend. It would be better to cancel the routine meeting altogether than to temporarily change it to a more convenient time for some of the members. Even if only two can gather, the continuity of the life of your little community will be preserved and you can be sure that Christ will be there to make it a threesome. Be assured that if your SCC is made to compete with other concerns and events, it will soon be viewed increasingly as draining like a dry, hot desert rather than the refreshing oasis it should be.

It is better to have too few meetings per month than too many. A gathering once a month is an ambitious goal for beginners. As SCC grows in the spirit of dialogue, it is easy to add on more frequent gatherings in keeping with the abilities and felt needs of the members.

Visitors to SCC

Another challenge to dialogue in SCC is the presence of visitors. It is ill advised to have more than one or two visitors and then usually on an exceptional basis. Your SCC needs the time to grow in faith, hope, and mutual love. You need private time for this to occur. Visitors would find it difficult to tap into the level of dialogue that your SCC has achieved. Without a doubt the visitor would enjoy the experience of a loving, concerned community. The danger is that the casual visitor will leave with the idea that it is easy to develop SCC. The visitor has not experienced the sweat and tears you have invested to make your community come alive.

It would be better, generally, to share your understanding of SCC with friends at times other than the time reserved for your SCC meeting. Obviously, a visitor must never be invited to observe your meeting as if you are on display. The visitor must be a participant because your endeavor is to touch life itself. There is no more sacred endeavor than to struggle to find oneself, neighbor, and God as an inseparable reality. Therefore, it is inconceivable that anyone should be just an observer.

Conclusion

We have thus far examined some strategies that are available for your gathering to set the stage for dialogue as well as salient obstacles to dialogue. Be aware that we can only set the environment for dialogue to occur. When it does occur and where it will lead is the work of the Spirit of God. Let us not be so presumptuous as to attempt control beyond setting the stage.

Even when we strive for the coming of the Holy Spirit by carefully preparing our SCC meeting down to every detail, our efforts may be derailed by insurmountable obstacles. We have touched on a few such barriers and given some suggestions on how to deal with them. Undoubtedly you are well aware of many more stumbling blocks toward achieving greater dialogue in your SCC. Bring them up in your SCC and share insights on how to cope with and eventually overcome them.

It is time to move on to the next chapter in which your SCC will be introduced to challenges that will test your ability to dialogue to the core. But first, let us recognize the amazing feat that you have hitherto accomplished. You have been meeting now for an extended period of time to form SCC. You have held together with one faith, hope, and caring love. Congratulations for accomplishing something many like to think about but few dare attempt. There is much more that could be said about the inner life of your SCC but the world could not hold all the books that would be written. You now have an identity as a unique gathering based on faith and hope. Be patient because you will grow in the years to come. You do not need all the answers to the inner life of SCC to plunge into it and to rejoice with each new discovery.

At this point perhaps, your SCC of 10 to 12 members has been meeting for a year. Don't feel that you must rush ahead on any timetable or schedule. There is plenty of material in this chapter that needs to be sorted out in order to prepare you for the arduous journey that will be unfolded in Chapter 3. The following questions and answers may be helpful to stimulate discussion that will help you grow in an understanding of dialogue within your SCC. These questions and answers will be followed by discussion questions that may be helpful in reviewing the content of this chapter.

QUESTIONS AND ANSWERS

Q. One of the members of our gathering is an outspoken "conservative" who feels threatened when the prayers or discussions stray from the straight and narrow. Some in our SCC want to push this person into dropping out. Should we?

A. Conformity in both behavior and spirit is the hallmark of a large group. An army, for example, would easily be defeated without strict conformity, and personal differences are de-emphasized as counterproductive to smooth functioning.

In a small community, however, the dynamic is quite different. In this setting, individual differences enhance the life of the community. The differences in personalities create interest and growth (sometimes painful) in each member. In SCC environment, it is certainly not productive, and is often even inaccurate, to place labels such as conservative, liberal, or moderate on members. Labels tend to isolate, divide, and often cause a breakdown of communication.

SCC, by definition, is designed to create a situation where everyone can fully belong, be themselves, and feel accepted by all. The very source of life for a small community is the struggle and resulting growth stemming from accepting a person as that person is. This goes both ways, of course. The community member you refer to also has to allow other members the same freedom. For all members this struggle is an exercise of faith (a plunging into the unknown). It is also an exercise of hope (celebrating new life following the struggle) that ultimately leads us to accept God who is totally different from us because God is the original initiator of love, that is, God was first to take us as we are. When we do the same to others we come to know God because we are becoming like our divine suitor.

It should be clear from this that it is inappropriate to manipulate anyone to either join or leave SCC. In such instances the manipulator would be harmed, and dialogue in the SCC would greatly suffer.

Q. We have a former priest and a former nun in our SCC. While they contribute a lot to discussions, they sometimes take control and inhibit members from sharing. What can we do?

A. First of all, remember that the people you are asking about are accustomed to being regarded as "religious leaders," and so they may be taking over unconsciously. Sometimes, all it takes is a private "aside" to point out to the person that he or she is taking over and inhibiting others.

On the other hand, your friends may be operating out of a false sense of what it means to lead. They might be confusing leadership with lecturing. It's easy to lecture a group because personal involvement is minimal. Entering into a discussion with a community is more difficult because the exchange of ideas leads to greater personal involvement. Dialoguing with others is by far the most difficult, since the level of communication touches on exchange of emotions and mutual acceptance of responsibility toward one another.

Anyone (not limited to priests and nuns) may try to dominate a group by lecturing since this requires the least amount of involvement. Skilled facilitators can provide a service to the lecturer, and at the same time reduce the tension in the SCC, by first listening attentively and then inviting other members to speak to the same issue raised by the lecturer. If "lectures" continue, repeat this exercise until there is a free-flow of discussion. If all else fails, move on as soon as possible to refreshments and informal discussions. The opportunity for private conversations will put a damper on the lecturer/audience framework.

Q. Our SCC has been meeting now for over a year for prayer and discussion. Should we assume that it's time to move on? How long should a small Christian community keep going?

A. The needs of the persons involved will determine how long a particular community stays in existence. Unlike large organizations, the small community of faith exists for the good of individual persons. Even if a given community ceases to meet, its life will continue forever if it has evoked new life in its members.

Some SCCs endure for years and years. Though the same people meet week after week, they recognize that each meeting is unique and each member is constantly changing and growing because of their daily life experiences.

Membership in SCC requires openness to such change and considerable discipline because its ultimate purpose is unselfish. The small community exists to help members become mature persons of faith. If a given community has lost sight of this goal, or if it is no longer open to change and growth, it will probably fall apart on its own. As long as it does encourage growth in faith, it can and should survive.

Q. There's a running argument among members of our prayer group. Some say we should focus on ourselves as individuals, and others think that the emphasis should be on how we function as a community. What do you think?

A. Your group members might recall that central to the Judeo-Christian tradition is the notion that God is in dialogue with people. Jesus is the word (dialogue) of God made flesh. Dialogue is by definition between two persons and only secondarily involves the community, as an overflow of person-to-person dialogue.

Community, therefore, is secondary, an effect, not a cause. Jesus has invited us as his disciples to enter into dialogue with the Father and the Holy Spirit, who will remind us of all that Jesus has said and done. As a consequence of our reflection on his words and deeds, we will be able to do works far greater that Jesus has done (John 14:12). This person-to-person dialogue is the ultimate source of all power in the church, a process reaching fullness in Jesus. It will continue until all his disciples are in communion with the Father. This event will constitute the end of time. In short, nothing happens in your community unless it first happens in the heart of one of your members. Therefore, it is clear that the only place good can overcome evil is within a person's heart. That is where the battle is and that is where the emphasis must be.

Q. One couple wants to bring their two young children to the small community meeting. Children inevitably become the center of attention. How do children fit into a small community?

A. Children will be tremendously influenced when exposed to a small community of faith. Before this can occur, however, a small community must be firmly established and well developed among adult members. Then the small community of faith will serve as an extended family to young children providing them with an ideal environment for absorbing Christian values.

To include small children, social activities should be planned that will be of interest to both adults and children. It should be made clear to the children that they are members of the small community and the general mixing at social events should serve to affirm this. Also, participation in baptisms, weddings and funeral will make the small community of faith real to children.

Q. How do teenagers fit into small communities?

A. In the time of Christ there weren't any people thought of as "teenagers," but only children and adults. At 12 years of age, Christ was presented at the temple signifying that he had become as adult member of his synagogue. Young people should be invited and made to feel welcome in small community discussions, sharing, liturgies and socializing activities. Threats or force are inappropriate as each person must be allowed and encouraged to develop at his or her own pace. Young adults can add a certain freshness to the life of a small community of faith.

Q. We have grown close during the months that we have met but one person has taken advantage of the openness of another member by "coming on to her." Both are married to some one else. What can we do in this situation?

A. You are touching on an explosive issue. Saint Paul rebuked the SCCs of his day for abusive displays of affection. Contrary to widespread belief, love and sex are not synonymous. In the Christian view, love and responsibility are two sides of the same coin. Thus, Christ loved even to the extreme of the cross. There is no greater love than to lay down one's life for a friend.

Remember that SCC is like a two-edged sword: growth in dialogue will increase the intimacy between married couples leading to greater joy and at the same time to greater capacity for pain should rejection by one of the partners occur. There is always the danger that a person may turn against the increasing growth and responsibility that comes with dialogue. When a spouse does so, joy melts away from the relationship and continued fidelity to the unwilling spouse leads to an agonizing pain for the one seeking deeper sharing of life.

Paul had no solution for the dissolving of espousal relationships, nor do we. SCC leads to ever deeper levels of dialogue and in so doing is going to cause pain for those who wish more shallow relationships devoid of responsibility. To be faithful to Christ, the members of SCC must continue to pursue responsibility for one another through a loving dialogue in order to reverse the anti-Christ attitude of the murderous Cain who rejected God with the defiant cry, "Am I my brother's keeper?"

While growth in SCC may occasion painful division and even separation, the SCC also has the power of Christ to heal. The Spirit of Christ that pours into SCC is easily recognized because it brings life and not death, love not abuse, light not darkness, hope not despair. In the context of this healing community we can grow to become more responsible for each member without being responsible for the choices made by a fellow member.

These remarks may not really answer the question, but we hope the reflections will help you to arrive at a solution for your situation.

Q. Our small community fell apart. My wife and I miss it very much and feel discouraged. How can we get things moving again?

A. Call or visit former members of your small community. Tell them how you feel and ask them to openly and honestly share their views about why your small community no longer wishes to come together any more. Then invite them to one more gathering to take stock of the situation. At the very least, all will learn a great deal about themselves and what it takes to make a small community of faith thrive. Perhaps, as a result, your small community will get a new lease on life.

There is always a danger of a small community of faith becoming comfortable with little or no giving on the part of the members. During at least one full session each year the community should take a good look at itself, identify potential problems, and agree upon a course of action to make corrections. This may be a painful process, but growth has never been guaranteed without pain.

QUESTIONS FOR REVIEW AND DISCUSSION

1. Why is dialogue more difficult when the community increases in size? Meets more frequently? Entertains visitors? Changes meeting dates for the convenience of a member?

2. Is diversity in the membership a help or a hindrance to the development of SCC? Explain.

3. What are some strategies for inducing growth in dialogue? What are the merits of each? Are they needed for a successful SCC?

4. What are major obstacles to dialogue? What obstacles have you found in yourself? In your SCC?

5. To find one true friend in a lifetime is an accomplishment of note. If this is so, is our pursuit of a genuine SCC an impossible dream? If so, should we pursue this goal faced with a lifetime of frustration? Is it healthy to do so? Is it healthy not to do so?

6. In what way is the Trinity a model for SCC? Is the Trinity a realistic model for SCC? Explain.

7. Why is it important for SCC to make its own decisions? How should decisions be made?

8. Are authority and influence identical? Does SCC have authority? Does SCC have influence? Explain.

9. What part does Scripture play in SCC? Are readings from more relevant modern authors more desirable than Scriptures for SCC discussion or liturgy?

10. What is prayer? How does prayer fit into the life of SCC?

Chapter 3

Spreading the Gospel

After spending a year with the first SCC, Jesus sends the members two by two to every town and village where he was to go. Jesus instructs them: "Take nothing for your journey but a staff, no wallet, no bread, no money in your belt; wear sandals and don't put on two tunics. Whenever you enter a house, stay there until you leave the town" (Mark 6:8-10).

From this Scripture passage we learn that the coming presence of Christ is announced in each town and village, not by a soul-stirring preacher arriving on the scene like a lone knight in shining white armor, but simply and humbly by members of a small community who had learned to dialogue after spending many months with Jesus in their midst.

No one to this day has improved on this method of spreading the gospel. If messengers of the gospel are not seen to be in dialogue, how can they speak of dialogue? Through dialogue, unity is possible and with unity all things are possible, as Christ points out: "Where even two on earth agree on something it will be done" (Mattthew 18:19). The remarkable unity achieved through dialogue, clearly evident in these SCCs formed by the first disciples of Jesus, is the method of proclaiming the coming presence of Christ not only in ancient times but also throughout history. Wherever even two come together in the name of Jesus, Christ is both made present and proclaimed to the world.

Dialogue as the Message

The first Christians believed dialogue to be so central to the gospel that they were told not to worry about life's other necessities, food, money, or extra clothing. Dialogue is the gateway to sharing whereby all other human needs will be met. Those individuals and institutions that seek power, wealth, or security first, do so because they do not have the true faith that underlies dialogue, the most critical need of every human heart and the underlying message that Jesus came to reveal.

Your little community, like countless thousands before it, has labored to enter into dialogue. Through this dialogue you have grown in faith and love, with Christ in your midst as initiator, teacher, healer, and purveyor of countless graces. In this chapter, we invite you to now shift your gaze away from the internal dialogical life of your SCC, the preoccupation of the former chapter, to an outward perspective through which we will examine how your SCC is affecting your environment.

We are not suggesting that you split up two by two to go to every village and town to proclaim that the kingdom of God has arrived. To repeat, the original missionary strategy of Christ is to spread the kingdom (that is, the influence of God) not by what you have to say, but by what you have become through dialogue. The original disciples were not sent out until they had entered into SCC relationship. The SCC itself is the message, not the words any member utters.

A community in dialogue is the sign to the world that Christ is indeed alive today and his healing spirit is at work.

During this past year while you concentrated on developing your SCC, your small community was generating a lot of influence on the world around you. In this chapter we direct your attention to the impact you are having on the surrounding world and the reactions you might expect.

No one lights a candle without producing light and heat. Your SCC, although ignited with a spark from Christ, the original light of the world, is, nevertheless something new in our world today. You can expect new light will shine from the gospels through your SCC, but also temperatures will rise with the friction generated. Recall that Jesus points out that when you light a lamp you place it on the mantle to give light to all in the house. Your SCC has been burning as a lamp giving light to the world.

Using another analogy, you might picture your SCC as a stone that has fallen into a still pond of water causing concentric circles of waves to spread out enveloping the entire pond. To put it as directly as possible, you cannot build SCC in a vacuum. There are many, many implications and consequences that you must be aware of and be prepared to deal with. To do this you need to take a look at the external environment of your SCC.

Inclusive vs Exclusive Love

Let us begin by reflecting on the inclusive love that has been the very life of your SCC for this past year. As you may recall, inclusive love within your SCC means that you have accepted each other with joy and allowed each to be his or her own unique person. You have learned to accept one another's strengths and weaknesses, unique perspectives and values. Each member, although very different—like the various parts of a body—still form the one body of Christ.

What has been viewed by the members of your SCC as inclusive love may be viewed by outsiders, who are aware of the existence of your SCC, as exclusive love. You have formed an "in group" that undoubtedly has made others feel uncomfortable and left out. Most will have no inclination to join your SCC, but nevertheless do feel its influence.

Because learning to dialogue is extremely difficult and can be done only when the community is small, group size must necessarily be limited. This means setting unpopular restrictions on the number of members in a given SCC. Outsiders can easily view the restriction as setting up an elitist group. In truth, members need a small community to learn inclusive love in order to practice inclusive love in the community as a whole. This exercise of inclusive love is the way Christ is made present in our time and place to bring about the redemption of all.

Do not make the mistake of expecting people outside your SCC to understand the meaning of the dialogue you are trying to learn or the inclusive love you carry from your SCC to the world. Christ was crucified because the religious leaders of the people felt that what he taught and did was disruptive and dangerous to the tribal harmony the religious leaders sought to preserve. Also, do not make the mistake of feeling that your SCC is any better than others. Any attempt to put yourself above others will only serve to confirm suspicions about your SCC.

SCC and the Pastor

With these introductory remarks, let us look at the immediate environment of your SCC. Obviously the pastor of the parish in which your meetings take place is going to be at least curious and, possibly, greatly concerned. How does a pastor of a parish relate to SCC? Your SCC must learn to extend the dialogue you have learned. Talk to your pastor. Keep him well informed. There is absolutely nothing secret in SCC development. Creating SCC is indeed difficult but secrecy has no place in an endeavor to develop dialogue.

Ideally, your pastor should be involved at the very beginning of SCC because inclusive love must be the spirit of SCC from the very beginning. Your pastor, who is viewed by many people as guide to religious belief and practice, has a legitimate interest and concern in something as important as SCC. But, do not expect your pastor to drop other important commitments in order to be at the beck and call of your SCC. His lack of involvement may not necessarily mean that he is not interested. Invite him to participate as much as possible. It is important that he be kept well informed about the progress of your small community of faith. If properly informed, he will likely become your strongest supporter.

In all likelihood, if your SCC pursues a life of inclusive love, your pastor will be drawn to you like an iron filing to a magnet. Initially, he will feel great distress because he will be torn by his concerns for the parish as a whole. He will feel divided, fearing that time spent with one small community diminishes the time and attention that should be devoted to the entire parish.

Be patient and aware that your pastor is head of a sizeable corporation with a multitude of activities. In some cases, this includes operation of a school, no small undertaking in these changing times. Undoubtedly your pastor's time is in great demand. However, you need not feel defensive in seeking his involvement in your SCC. He too needs to enter into dialogue as a way of life, and he needs to do it with people who do not relate to him as administrators, heads of organizations, or project coordinators. He needs to discover and rediscover what constitutes a living, effective Christian community in our modern world. You can provide him with that experience and in so doing give him a vision for directing all other parish activities.

You may wonder how the life in one SCC can set the tone for an entire parish. This leads us to the greatest enigma of all time: large communities are small, while small communities are large. You can easily be lost in a large community like a parish because the larger the size the more superficial is the involvement that is required. Small communities have much greater leadership potential because a small community requires an ever increasing measure of personal involvement precisely because it is small. Thus, it follows that if you seek the greatest God of all, seek that God in the smallest of all, where personal involvement is greatest. Your pastor will find God, not by being the ruler of a large enterprise, but, as you did, by being the least in SCC. God is drawn to and through the least, not the greatest among us (Luke 9:48).

SCC and the Parish Structure

A word of caution is in order at this point. Some newcomers to SCC use the occasion to react against organized religion as the enemy of the spirit of free religious expression. You may have already worked through this reactionary phase in your SCC. However, be patient with members reacting to structures. The SCC needs the parish and its universal and historical traditions. In chapter five we will look in some depth at SCC in its historical perspective at which time the need for parish and parish structure will be more apparent. For the moment, as we try to define the relationship SCC has with organized religion, concretized in your pastor and parish structures, it is sufficient to point out that your SCC, while it will bring abundant new life to a parish, nevertheless needs the anchor provided by parish structure. The goal of union with God and neighbor through the dialogue that you seek is by no means an easy one. As a rule of thumb, apply the admonition Jesus gave the SCCs which he started: "Whoever is not against us is for us" (Mark 9:39).

As your SCC begins to look outward in this chapter, be aware that you must constantly work very hard on forming the right attitude toward your parish. The structure of the parish is there to support not discourage your efforts. The parish itself is by definition a Christian community. It makes sense to view your parish as a community of SCCs in the same way your diocese is a community of smaller (parish) communities. If yours is the only SCC in your parish, don't feel discouraged. Remember that the longest journey begins with the first step. Do not be afraid to see your SCC as a form of organized religion with definite structure, members, meeting times, strategies for dialogue, and purpose. Your SCC, however, is infinitely more than a human structure. Truth is found in the balance of the visible with the invisible. It would be impossible to drink from a vast ocean of water without a small cup to scoop up a little. Your SCC is as a small ladle which enables you to scoop up from the ocean of grace God has made manifest in Jesus the Beloved. As members of your SCC grow in faith and love, the entire parish will feel the overflow effects.

SCC and the Parish Council

Keeping your pastor involved and informed as you develop your SCC is not enough. You must also become knowledgeable regarding parish organizations and projects. Many parishes have a board or council that oversees all aspects of parish life from such mundane concerns as sweeping and locking the parish plant to initiating programs for spiritual enrichment of parishioners.

You can expect that during the past year your SCC has been discussed a number of times in the parish council meeting and for good reason. The SCC movement throughout the world is not just another organization. It has the potential to shift the emphasis in parish life away from church as a building to church as a people. Such a development will have profound implications for your parish council.

Do not adopt a defensive approach by trying to sell SCC to your parish council. Your parish council is already aware of your efforts because it is impossible to build SCC in a vacuum. Your influence has already been felt by parish leaders. These leaders, understandably, may be hesitant to give positive response initially because they may be fearful that your SCC is only the latest fad to come along and has little substance.

Here again patience is needed. Do not make the mistake of assuming a hostile or critical attitude to every question or observation directed toward your SCC. Show a willingness to become interested and involved in the concerns and projects of your parish leaders and in due time you will influence them to become more interested in SCC. Keep parish leaders informed about what you are doing. To repeat, secrecy has no place in SCC where our struggle to become aware of our calling to be the beloved of God is carried on at its most intense level.

Most parish councils have a spiritual life committee. At the very least, your SCC can make a connection with parish structure through this committee. An effective linkage with one committee of the parish council will provide an avenue of communication to all other committees of the parish and ultimately to all parishioners. If misunderstandings or harmful rumors arise in the parish regarding SCC, you will be in a position to respond in a timely and healing way through established channels of communication.

SCC and Parishioners

This brings us to yet another dimension of influence. Consciously or unconsciously your SCC has been influencing parishioners in general. This dimension includes also the wider circle of acquaintances, family, and friends. You may not be aware of it, but during this past year participation in the faith life of SCC has brought about profound changes in you that will be noticed by the people with whom you associate. Some may be amused, others may react strongly to the changes.

These changes may include such things as need for more meaningful conversations, greater interest in the local community or national or world affairs, deeper understanding of Scripture and religious practices, or a happier, lighter heart generally. Amusement of your friends can easily give way to annoyance and, in time, to harsh criticism or even rejection.

For some members of SCC, the disruption of long-standing relationships may be very difficult to bear.

Make no mistake about it, SCC is going to be like a stone in a shoe for a faceless, impersonal parish or society in general. While your SCC does not wish to be the cause of pain, sometimes it is unavoidable. SCC can be like the rush of blood into an arm or leg that has fallen asleep. When circulation is restored the painful experience subsides. In like manner, when your reacting friends are drawn into the deeper level of dialogue that you are experiencing, the formerly comfortable but dormant relationship with old friends will be transformed and will take on new life.

When and how the life-giving blood of dialogue will circulate in your parish, family, or in society at large is ultimately in the hands of God. We are not the initiators of the effort. Adam disrupted dialogue with God leading as a consequence to fratricide with the blood of Abel on the hands of Cain. Angry blood has continued to flow to our own day. Since the time of Adam, God has taken the initiative to restore communion. We are privileged to share in God's work but are not privy to the total picture. Christ caused pain in the conscience of many and as a result became a target upon which pain was inflicted. We who try to follow in his footsteps cannot expect to be treated differently.

Dealing with Hostility

There is no easy answer to solving reactions from those who feel excluded from your SCC. Limits to the size of SCC must be set if dialogue is to be preserved. Regardless of how much inclusive love you extend to persons outside your SCC, suspicions and misunderstandings are inevitable. It is helpful if you are cognizant that agony and ecstasy are often two sides of the same coin. Regardless of the ridicule or rejection, you cannot compromise the demands of the gospel in order to please those who may be offended by your participation in SCC.

Be aware that many people inadvertently demand a tribal sameness as the basis of unity for family, friends, or church. If indeed you are a unique person and your SCC is consequently unique, absolute sameness would require violence to attain. Small community with sameness is a definition of a gang, not a community of faith where violence has no place. If you set SCC as an ideal to attain, differences not sameness will be the source of life and peace.

Thus, SCC is not a haven for the fainthearted. We gather in SCC not as a "support group," but precisely because we are strong. We want to do something about the discord and bloodshed we see everywhere in our world. When we set things right in our small community of faith and love by valuing persons more than we value differences between persons, we are in the process of setting things right in the world. In so doing, however, we must be strong enough to bear the consequences. When you turn on the light, lovers of dark deeds will be very unhappy.

While a direct answer to outside pressures opposed to SCC is not feasible, an indirect approach through expanding the number of SCCs in your parish is possible. Let us assume your SCC has been meeting three or four hours on the last Sunday of each month for a year or more. You have come to realize that your SCC must "act" rather than react to your outside environment. Your constructive influence on the total community could be increased by members of your SCC initiating other small communities on some other day of the month other than on the last Sunday on which your primary community has chosen to meet. There is no objection to being a member of more than one SCC. As more and more SCCs develop in the community, hostile reactions will inevitably melt by the collective influence of inclusive love from the SCCs in the area.

Another indirect approach is to have your entire SCC meet with a larger group at some other time during the month in order to provide an experience of community (i.e. the sense of satisfaction that comes with constructive involvement in dialogue about important issues). Use the strategies you have learned in SCC to bring about meaningful dialogue in a larger group. From this larger group other SCCs can be formed.

One final caution as your SCC looks out at the surrounding environment: Do not fall into the mistake of developing a bunker mentality. By coming together and sharing your faith in the presence of Christ, you are doing a great service not only to one another in your SCC but to the entire community. You are a healing cell in a society torn by the cancer of selfishness because you are making Christ live again through your humble efforts. So make no apology. Stand firm for what you believe in, as the disciples of Christ did of old.

Conclusion

Let's look back at where we have been before we direct our gaze at the new horizons of the next chapter. Even when only two of your SCC members came together in the name of Christ, Christ was always there to make it a threesome. Although you cannot see him with your eyes, you feel his presence because he sets the tone and substance of the dialogue that occurs. As you find yourself being transformed by the dialogue, you have evidence that the Spirit of Christ indeed continues to abide with you.

In the first chapter you labored to achieve the goal of being SCC with just two members. You learned that the context of your gathering and growth in dialogue are the essential ingredients.

In the second chapter you took the giant step of expanding dialogue to include more people in your SCC. You learned that adding more members does not in any way change the importance or sacredness of SCC. The step was not one of diluting the level of dialogue achieved or converting it into superficial socializing, but one of plunging into an infinitely more complex endeavor aimed at achieving the level of dialogue found in the Blessed Trinity, the central truth of Christian doctrine and the prototype par-excellence of SCC.

Finally, in the third chapter we tried to make meaningful connections with the outside world. Your SCC, if it is to reflect Christ, then, like Christ, it is to be in the world even though your SCC aspires to a deeper world.

Chapters 4, 5, and 6 will focus on the SCC as the mediator between this world and the world that is coming, a world briefly glimpsed 2000 years ago in Christ. To mediate the new world, the SCC must fulfill its divine calling to reflect Jesus the Beloved (Christ) as priest, prophet, and kingly-servant. When we are instructed by Paul to put on Christ, he is referring to putting on Christ as priest (worship), prophet (understanding), and kingly servant (inclusive love put into action). Chapters 4 to 6 will focus on each of these dimensions of Christ's presence in the world and will dwell on the implications of SCC as vehicles of God's transforming and redeeming grace. By understanding each of these dimensions of SCC, it is our hope that your SCC will have gained the insight on how to continue on your own to achieve the unique calling you have to be emmanuel (God with us) in our world today.

Before we launch into the new world that SCCs herald, it may be helpful for your SCC to discuss certain issues raised in the form of questions and answers pertaining to how your SCC relates to its external environment. This can be followed by a discussion of a series of questions aimed at reviewing the salient points of this chapter.

QUESTIONS AND ANSWERS

Q. My friend in another city is interested in belonging to a small Christian community. His parish is very large (2200 families). He asked the pastor if he would consider convening such a group, but the pastor is too busy with other parish concerns. Should my friend try to start a small faith community himself?

A. By all means, yes. Explain to your friend that every small community of faith begins (and continues) with the initiative of an individual. Someone must initiate an invitation to which others can respond. But first your friend needs to reflect carefully on the implications of entering into the ministry of inviting. By inviting he is not only responding to the invitation of God to fuller life, but is also learning the cost of personal involvement.

It will be easy to proceed when the response of others is yes, but there will also be negative or indifferent responses. These will cause him pain and frustration and thus he must rely on the strength that comes from God. He should start by meeting with one other interested person and gradually invite others to join him. He should set a time, place, and agenda judged to be acceptable to those invited. Then, from the first meeting on, he can let the SCC plan its own future.

Q. One of our members is a highly motivated social activist and would like the rest of us to get on the bandwagon. We admire her zeal, but should our small community become a social action group?

A. A good Christian community serves primarily as a sanctuary where we have the opportunity to get our bearings in the modern world. We need the understanding and encouragement of others to sort out our values and to make decisions accordingly. Once we've made such decisions, we are ready to engage in social action, either on our own or in union with others, but not necessarily with members of our SCC.

Jesus' comment that the poor will always be with us (Matthew 26:11) should not be used to justify indifference to the poor or to other social action agendas. Jesus himself was wholly dedicated to those in need, and he promised that giving even a cup of cool water to one in need would be rewarded. Jesus insisted, however, that his followers first have a right heart and right head. This is the primary function of SCC. A small faith community should continue to offer spiritual nurture so that social action can follow, but such action is not the central concern of SCC.

Q. I am on the parish council and belong to the Knights of Columbus. Why would I want to be in a small faith community?

A. A small community of faith is unique because its sole purpose is growth in the life of faith. The parish council, the Knights of Columbus, and other parish circles and clubs have a different focus, such as parish decision making, social action, entertainment, education, or community service.

Small faith communities are based on the recognition that faith is a growth process that passes through a number of stages. The faith of members may only be at the beginning point like a small mustard seed, or their faith might have already grown into a large tree that can offer shelter to birds that land in it branches (Matthew 13:31). SCC provides the opportunity to nurture growth in faith at all levels. As such, it stands as a unique institution, it is the church at its most basic level.

Q. My husband does not go to any church but wants to be a part of our small community. Should I encourage him to go to church?

A. Vatican II defines the church as a dialogue. Your husband apparently is attracted to the experience of dialogue that is the very life of a small community of faith. When he sees this occurring in larger church gatherings, he will feel the attraction. Any effort to push will only invite a negative reaction and therefore slow down the growth process.

Q. Our small community has grown to 20 adult members. Should we split into two communities?

A. The wishes of those involved must be the basis of any decision affecting the community. A small gathering of 10 to 12 adults is needed to insure that everyone is heard to a minimal degree. A variety of strategies can be utilized to achieve this. Sub-groups can be formed for part of a meeting and rejoined for a general session. In another strategy, part of a small community may meet on one day and part on another day, followed by a joint meeting at another time. Again, to reduce the size of a community, some may wish to form a nucleus to join with new members to start a new community of faith. Each community should design a strategy that best fits its need to achieve an ever deeper level of dialogue.

Q. We belong to a small parish in a small town where everyone knows everyone else. What could development of small communities add?

A. Getting to know someone is only the first step toward delving into the meaning of a community experience. SCC seeks to make visible the mystery of the church that leads to communion with God and neighbor. In doing so, we follow the lead of Christ, the first to be a neighbor to the degree that God is perfectly reflected in the relationship. Getting to know another person progresses through many stages from the most superficial to the deepest levels of communication.

Martha knew Christ at the social level of sharing a meal with him. Mary, her sister, knew him at a deeper level of sharing the word of life with him. Regardless of how well you know a person, there is always more to know and appreciate. Love will stimulate the process of revelation. In this same process, a person will come to a greater knowledge and understanding of him or herself. Knowledge must then be turned into love, for this is the essence of a Christian's call to holiness (or wholeness). Knowledge without love leads to tyranny.

Q. We live in a small town and have witnessed the gradual

introduction of drugs from a large city some miles distant. The drugs are accompanied by increases in violence, gangs, break-ins, rape, and a host of other crimes associated with drug use. How would small community structure in our parish help to stop this social cancer?

A. "Social cancer" is an apt description of drug abuse. The individual uses these substances to obtain a "high" or individual "experience" that cuts one off or isolates one person from another. The individual's behavior is like a cancerous cell that lives isolated from the other cells in the body and begins devouring neighboring cells until the whole organism dies. Small communities enable members to resist behaviors destructive to the community as a whole. Illicit use of drugs is one of these destructive activities that bring only harm to the total community.

The small community also provides a "high" that consists in a surge of life experience for the individual as well as the total SCC. Unlike drugs, where after the first "high," there is a gradual decline ending in depression and despair, the experience of life in a faith community increases in levels of joy and ends with unimaginable peace. In short, we need not sit still wringing our hands in despair as we see our country being destroyed by drugs. Development of small communities of faith and concern for neighbor will lead to a reconstruction beginning in neighborhoods, and extend into small towns, cities, and ultimately to the country as a whole. A well developed community will afford healing to those victimized by drugs.

Q. Isn't there such a thing as psychological drugs and aren't they as dangerous as chemical drugs?

A. There are such things as psychological drugs and they can be even more dangerous than chemical drugs because they are harder to recognize. The most pervasive psychological drug is that of using God or Jesus as a drug to solve every problem or emergency instead of taking individual responsibility.

God has given us power to take charge of our own lives. In SCC, members are called upon to do precisely that. A faceless Christian is a contradiction in terms. Each must take the responsibility of being called as unique persons to be in a special way in dialogue with God—as was Jesus. Many, in an effort to avoid pain that comes with growth or in some way to dodge responsibility, turn to God or religion as an escape drug of choice rather than as a challenge to be true to themselves.

In his book, *When God Becomes a Drug*, Leo Booth provides a twelve-step recovery plan for those whose approach to God and religion is that of a drug addict. The danger of psychological drug addiction was well illustrated some years ago when the Rev. Jim Jones induced his many unquestioning followers to take poison so that they could be together in another world. Sadly, those addicted to any drugs, chemical or psychological, are missing out on the real world and the loving God who seeks dialogue with us through it.

Q. My husband and I and another couple have been gathering together about once a month for two years. We began with a slightly larger group during Lent, using a program our parish provided. Now we use a booklet for discussion and prayer. We enjoy this time together but feel the need to grow in numbers. Do you have any suggestions on how we do this? How is a group built from the ground floor? I would like to see more material written on groups just beginning. I feel overwhelmed reading about SCCs that have been meeting for years and are well established. At the same time, I want their spirituality and intimacy for my own faith community.

A. Three questions are raised here that should be answered separately: 1) How do you start a small community? 2) How do you expand a small community to include new members? 3) How does a community achieve intimacy?

Answers to these questions should be prefaced with a clear understanding of the religious education most Catholics in the

Western world have received. Many have learned about their church as something outside themselves and consequently have grown up with the church at arms length. "Church" is associated with Sunday, building, hierarchy, Mass, sacraments, weddings, funerals, and weekly contributions. "Community" is seen as frosting on the cake.

Emphasis on small communities seems to change all of this by bringing church close to home, so to speak. Smaller size forces us to look more deeply into what a faith community is all about. Small community brings involvement with others, dialogue on issues of doctrine and morals to gain understanding, sharing of experiences, growth toward greater spiritual intimacy with God in communion with one's neighbor. In a large community, individual involvement can remain on a very superficial level. Most are not ready for this profound shift in emphasis, but prefer to see religion as a highly individual matter that one is to learn about but best keeps private.

With this background, answers to the three questions are easier to understand.

1. Begin a small community by making a decision that this is the path to God that you are choosing for yourself as a way of life (your resolve will be thoroughly tested as you seek to find the way). Then do the obvious things such as: get assistance from your parish priest, make announcements in the weekly bulletin, contact people that you know may be interested, have them contact their friends. If all else fails, put an ad in the local newspaper. Get people together and brainstorm for ideas. Begin with social activities and, in time move on to discussion, then to prayer, liturgy, and sharing when the gathering is ready. Do not allow any attitude to develop that suggests that participants are superior to others. It is simply a matter of finding those who want more than what they had in the past which often meant participation in large groups operating at a more superficial level.

2. It is difficult for beginners to join SCC that has been

meeting for two years. Perhaps the veterans could continue to meet, but in addition each couple could head up new SCCs so that most will be at the beginning stages.

3. Intimacy reflects the level of personal not community development. A community will remain forever superficial unless one or more of its members enters into the aesthetics of spiritual development. The best guide for SCC development is that provided by the gospels. The four gospels originated from small gatherings of early Christians who wanted to preserve for all time how small communities of believers are to reflect the authentic spirit of Christ. The gospels provide a four-dimensional view so that all can easily understand what a small community must be to make Christ present in the world.

Q. I have been appointed by the pastor to start small communities in the parish. How do I get started? I need all the help I can get.

A. Unfortunately, no one has all the answers to developing small faith communities. The ministry involved in forming SCCs is a way of life that involves an endless commitment with a vision that SCCs will become the primary expression of church for the foreseeable future. There is a rapidly increasing volume of literature on SCC that can be very helpful. Available literature together with your own resourceful imagination will provide you with the creative ideas you need as well as point out what will lead to frustration, success, or failure.

Also, get other parishioners involved. You will gain a lot of ideas and encouragement from people who share your vision. Above all, avoid all short cuts or crash programs. It is very important to retain a long-range view because it may be well into the next century before the church generally achieves the ability to function at the personal level of small faith communities. In the meantime, take time to relish the challenge and excitement of being a pioneer in introducing the church into the world today.

Q. Our family had to move for job-related reasons. We really miss the small community experience of our former parish. Our new parish has nothing. My husband is angry about it. What should I do?

A. Whenever possible, return to meet with your original small community of faith or at least stay in touch. Encourage your husband to express his feelings of frustration and anger to your original community, which is much more likely to understand. This will provide great relief to your husband and will help his original community to appreciate the growth it has achieved.

This is a time of continued growth for all but especially for your husband. He moved from the small faith community with the unwarranted assumption that all members of his faith have had the same experience and share the same values as he does. He must now painfully mature to an awareness that he must accept the commitment of building up a small community as a personal lifestyle, independent of the response of others. In other words, he is being called to be a leader instead of a follower. Be patient and do not lose hope. In the last analysis, your husband must make this decision in his own heart.

One final word of caution: do not be too hard on your new pastor. He has been trained to administer a large parish. Small faith community is a new experience for him, too. Give him time. The chances are he is too busy to even think about small communities. Invite him over for dinner and talk to him about your vision for the church. In so doing a seed will be planted that will bear fruit in good time.

Q. I am confused. People refer to a small faith gathering as a group, circle, meeting, church, discussion club, assembly, and who knows what else. Can you put a label on this development in the church?

A. This issue is an excellent topic for discussion in a small gathering as a way of defining what it is that the gathering is all about. The sensitivity of each person obviously needs to be considered in arriving at a label.

The word "group" emphasizes organization and action; for example, dividing into groups to attain an objective. "Circle" and "club" generally emphasize discussion and social activity. "Church," as we have seen, comes from the Greek word for "assembly" and signifies simply a "calling together." When people respond to the call, that is when they form "church," it is then possible to pray, worship, discuss, plan social action, or simply grow as persons of faith as a result of the coming together. Each gathering, however small, can be viewed as a microcosm of the universal call to become church.

The development of SCC in the church today is new to most people. However, the movement to small domestic churches that is occurring today throughout the world may best be understood as a return to our roots dating back to apostolic times. For hundreds of years the only form of church people knew was gathering in small communities in the homes of believers to share the letters from the apostles and to share their own growth in faith and love.

Q. Our pastor opposes the small community of faith development because he feels it would detract from Sunday contributions. Does this in fact occur?

A. When people belong to small Christian communities, the parish collection usually increases, and there is also an increase of participation in religious education, membership on parish boards, visitation of shut-ins, and social welfare activities. When we achieve inclusive love, as noted at the beginning of this chapter, all other needs are met. That is why the first SCCs sent out by Christ could go without the money, bread, change of clothes, and other provisions that we deem so important for our security. Where inclusive love exists, material goods will be in abundant supply.

Q. A member of our small faith community died recently and her funeral was held in the parish church, but our SCC feels we should have done something more. Do you have any suggestions?

A. Your deceased friend leaves a great emptiness in your small gathering that needs to be addressed. Have a service for your friend in your SCC. Remember that the influence of the departed continues in the lives of the loved ones that remain. This influence should be defined by each member of your SCC and celebrated with thanksgiving. No greater honor could be given to the deceased, and the emptiness you now feel will give way to deeper bonds among your members. In these bonds your friend continues to live and be an important part of your lives.

Plan the service in advance. It should at least consist of appropriate readings, the sharing of experiences of the deceased, and a shared meal. All will be amazed at how much healing grace can be drawn out of death if your SCC can turn what seems to be an abrupt ending into a new beginning.

Q. Our pastor joined our SCC because he felt it was important to experience this before encouraging others to become involved. However, this has led to envy by other groups in the parish. What should we do?

A. You are fortunate to have a pastor who realizes the need for personal growth in faith afforded by the dialogue in a small community. You are especially fortunate to have a pastor who wants to be a leader instead of a follower by first doing himself what he will be asking others to do in the future.

It is extremely short sighted on the part of other parishioners to envy your group. They should know that the clergy has no corner in the market on faith because God does not play favorites. God favors each and every one of us because in God's eyes we are all equally loved beyond all measure. If the parishioners can overcome this short-sighted envy, they will soon have a pastor who has rediscovered the excitement of the gospels. His new enthusiasm will quickly show up in Sunday homilies that are much more alive and in tune with the needs of the church today. Everyone will benefit from the faith nurtured by your SCC.

Q. A high school senior from a very nice family in our small town recently committed suicide. The whole town is confused and heart-broken. Does the small community of faith have any answers?

A. Suicide is among the leading causes of death among young people in the United States today. It seems to be a rising epidemic. When it occurs in your community it is shocking, especially since we assume that a high school senior has an exciting world of choices and is driven by lofty dreams. When suicide is chosen, it is astonishing and dreadfully final.

The issue is too complex for a brief explanation. Small faith communities make possible a sharing of our daily lives in the context of the gospel. A joy or pain shared in the unfolding life of SCC becomes a source of grace to all. Does it not make a lot of sense that teenagers, who are at the stage of outgrowing their natural family, however wholesome that family may be, should have a family of faith to help them take their first big steps into a larger, more complex world? Every effort ought to be made to include young people in the ongoing dialogue of your SCC so that their dreams are nurtured and lives of quiet desperation are healed. This is perhaps the best insurance against the young person opting for the final dreadful choice of suicide.

One more word of caution: a suicide is very much like a virus that can easily spread in a community. The antidote is the dialogue that is the life blood of SCC. Whatever you do, do not remain idle toward the dangerous virus that has been introduced in your midst. This is a time for action, not one of passively waiting for the influence of your SCC to be felt.

What must be done is to increase the level of dialogue in the community as a whole. Plan conferences, events, celebrations, activities, or anything to draw the people together so that the level of dialogue is enhanced. Increasing the intensity of dialogue is analogous to increasing the blood supply to the body allowing it to drive out a dangerous virus.

Q. We have a Lutheran couple in our small community who seem more Roman Catholic than some of our Catholic members. Should we try to get this couple to become Catholic?

A. There are more things that unite Catholics and Lutherans than divide. Unfortunately, for too many centuries we have emphasized what divides. The small faith community is an ideal setting for exploring elements of faith that are held in common. From this sharing, an environment is created to reflect with patience and love on sensitive issues that divide us. If your Lutheran friends choose to become Catholics, fine. If not, fine. This is between God and them and you should not coerce them in any way.

Remember that it is God who is the only source and author of unity for humankind. By our mutual efforts we try to create an atmosphere of loving acceptance so that the Spirit of God will have a chance to work and bring about the unity Christ intends. Furthermore, keep in mind that there can be no lasting unity or understanding on the regional, national or international level without first starting on the level of small faith community.

Q. I love my small community and have experienced tremendous growth through it. One of my friends hurt me deeply when she referred to it as a cult. How should I respond?

A. "Cult" is short for "culture." When a group begins to develop a private culture that is radically different or hostile to the general culture of a given society, the group is suspiciously labeled a "cult." This behavior encourages a tendency of viewing the group's activities as analogous to a cancerous cell that is disruptive to the other cells that work for the good of the whole body. When Christianity began, there were hundreds of cults throughout the Roman empire. Christianity survived because it saw itself as the fulfillment of 2000 years of Old Testament history. Small Christian communities must not allow themselves to be cut off from the total community. They must labor, and be seen to be doing so, to be the continuation of 2000 years of a great tradition. If people still persist in calling your community a cult in spite of your efforts to be a healthy cell building up the whole body of Christ, take heart in remembering that you are not the first nor will you be the last one to be target of a hostile stone.

Q. One member of our small community insists that we all must become active in social issues (e.g., homeless, food pantries, child abuse) or we don't deserve to be called a "church." What do you think about this?

A. No group can earn the title of "church." It is not an honorary degree. The word was coined 500 years before Christ to refer to the "act of coming together." Therefore, whenever two or more choose to come together, that act can be referred to as simply an act of "church." Thus, churches existed hundreds of years before Christ. When we speak of Christ starting a church, we are referring to Christ setting the depth of communion we should seek as we come together. The depth he has set is reflected in his broken body and spilt blood as he lovingly poured out his life for his small community of disciples. Whenever two or more decide to come together to strive for the standard Christ set, the act is properly referred to as a "Christian" church.

Tell your friend that your very act of coming together in a small faith community is in itself the beginning of a healing process that will in due time influence society to be concerned for its weakest members rather than its strongest. When that finally occurs, social problems will be corrected because the root cause, namely, refusal to be concerned for our brothers and sisters as our other self, will have been eradicated. Refusing to identify SCC as a social action group should not be taken to mean, however, that individuals need not take it upon themselves to become actively involved in social issues.

Q. My friend and I would like to start a small community of faith. Should we approach the pastor to get his permission?

A. If you do, be prepared for your pastor to faint. By baptism you were brought into a faith community and given the right to someday be the creator of a family of faith, just as at birth you received life and the right to someday pass it on through a family of your own. The shock may be too much for your pastor to hear parishioners wanting to take their baptism seriously. He is probably more conditioned to the experience of parishioners stampeding out of Mass to make room for the next crowd each Sunday. A major drawback of being baptized as an infant is that we have never been exposed to the meaning of baptism as a commitment to live our faith as a communitarian phenomenon. Many people erroneously think of their Christian faith as isolated from community in an individualized manner, me and God.

Tell your pastor about your plans for a small community. After he revives, invite him to participate because he received the same baptism that you and your friend did. Your pastor can be a great help in interesting other parishioners in your faith community. Before you even take the first step, however, bear in mind that what you are setting out to do is not a temporary project but a commitment to a way of life promised for you by your sponsors at baptism but now maturing to the point of being a decision that is your own.

Q. Our small community would like to have a joint meeting with a small faith community from another city or diocese in order to get new ideas on how to develop and grow. How do we contact other small communities?

A. Call your diocesan chancery office to inquire whether your diocese has an office of small community ministries. If so, the coordinator of the office can easily put you in touch with other small faith communities in the diocese. If your chancery does not have such an office, a letter from your small community or your pastor requesting this type of ministry could be very effective.

If you wish also to get in touch with small communities in other dioceses, make your request known to the small community office of those dioceses. Effort is still at the beginning stages for coordinating regional or national networks of small communities of faith. One such effort is that of Buena Vista (Box 5474, Arvada, Colorado, 80005). The growth of small community sharing has been strictly a grassroots development. However, national, regional, diocesan and parish structures are already in place and should be used as much as possible by SCCs.

QUESTIONS FOR REVIEW AND DISCUSSION

1. Draw an organizational chart of your parish. How does your SCC fit in? Should SCC be at the bottom or the top of the organizational chart? Explain.

2. Does SCC aggravate or alleviate the chronic shortage of priests? Does SCC make more work for your pastor or less? Explain.

3. How would you explain your SCC to your pastor? Parish council? Another parishioner? Friend?

4. What is the difference between exclusive and inclusive love? Be specific.

5. Should all SCCs be the same? Do differences create problems? Be specific.

6. Why did Jesus send his disciples two by two to every village to which he was going? Why were extra provisions for their journey unnecessary?

7. Why must SCC be formed in the context of the larger community and not in isolation from it?

8. Why must SCC make every effort to be open and avoid even the appearance of secrecy?

9. Which would be better, SCC member who reacts strongly to organized religion or SCC member who is indifferent?

10. What is meant by the enigmatic statement that a large community is small whereas a small community is large?

Chapter 4

This Is My Beloved

Shortly before Jesus' death, through which he makes his passage into the new world that he proclaims, he takes members of the first SCC, Peter, James, and John, with him to Mt. Tabor to give them a foretaste of what is coming. While gathered together on the mountain, the disciples observe the face of Jesus becoming radiant and his garments turning white as snow. Suddenly, Moses and Elijah join the gathering and begin entering into dialogue with Jesus. While Jesus is conversing, yet another voice joining in the dialogue is heard coming from the heavens declaring, "This is my beloved, hear him!" (Matthew 17:2).

The disciples are overwhelmed, but Peter, anxious to prolong the event as long as possible, finds voice to express his excitement by suggesting that he immediately set up three tents, one for Moses, another for Elijah, and a third for Jesus. The words are hardly out of his mouth when the experience is over. While descending from the mountain, Jesus cautions his little community not to reveal what occurred until people are ready for it.

New Covenant

Jesus is presented in this event on Mt. Tabor in dialogue with Moses, mediator of an old human-divine covenant based on the ten commandments. Jesus is also seen in dialogue with Elijah who it was said had never tasted death but who had been taken up to heaven in a fiery chariot. From ancient times it was believed that Elijah would return at the advent of a new world. The voice from heaven enters the dialogue announcing the inauguration of the new world that consists of a new covenant between God and humankind in the words, "This is my beloved!"

Moses, the great lawgiver, joins the SCC thus signifying that the old tribal covenant with God as chieftain and giver of laws is ending. Henceforth, God's relationship with us can be understood now in espousal terms: This is my beloved. Elijah joins the SCC on Mt. Tabor, thus signifying that the new world Jesus introduces spans both sides of the grave. Death has lost its grip on humankind.

Jesus is introducing a new priesthood that is to be the gateway to the new order that is beginning on Mt. Tabor. The essence of that priesthood is recognition of one's divine election as the beloved, followed by celebration of this unbelievable good fortune with an explosion of gratitude (eucharist), and, finally, invitation to all the world to accept the dignity conferred by God on each and every one. Through the exercise of this new priesthood, people are to be drawn into the new order when they are ready to hear.

The revelation overwhelmed Peter, James, and John and it continues to overwhelm us to this very day. An espousal relationship with the living God is absolutely mind- and heart-exploding. The dignity to which each of us is called is so incomprehensible that no word or image in this world can capture the reality; hence we are faced with the beginning of a new world that reaches beyond human imagination.

Because images fail to capture the designs of God, the entire universe itself now proclaims what God has been about since time began—as disclosed by Christ on Mt. Tabor. The central truth of Tabor is that God, in truth, has freely chosen each of us as "beloved." As God with Jesus this election draws us into dialogue through which we are gradually transformed. We experience a gradual transformation inwardly and a transfiguration outwardly in our lives as we respond to God's call.

Radical View of Worship

True worship of God consists of an ever increasing personal depth of saying yes, I do, to the divine proposal. Thus, the notion of worship offered to God has radically changed. In ancient times, divine worship consisted in making ritualistic offerings to God to placate God for offenses, to influence God to bestow favors, such as abundant crops, or to thank God for gifts received. Hitherto, divine worship was directed to a powerful, just, benevolent, sometimes vengeful, but always distant God.

Although many still cling to these ancient views, this notion of worship is no longer adequate. After Mt. Tabor, the only worship worthy of God is that of accepting God's espousal proposal. As one slowly opens the eyes of faith to this unutterable reality, the divine spouse transforms the beloved inwardly and evidence is detected in a transfiguration of the individual's features outwardly. This transformation and transfiguration visibly occurs in Jesus, the high priest of the new order, as he gathers with his small community of faith on Mt. Tabor. This same exercise of priesthood is occurring wherever SCCs gather in response to the voice from heaven: "This is my beloved."

Transition to a radically new perception of worship is very, very difficult for many, to say the least. It may help to reflect on what should be obvious, namely that God who created us and all things in the first place, does not need anything we have. We cannot do or give anything to God that God does not have already but with one exception. The only thing beyond the power of God to obtain is our acceptance of the espousal proposition offered. Thus, God can be worshipped only by our actual accepting the espousal relationship proposed, because only in this way can we truly give to God.

We may find it hard to fathom such one-sided generosity. The problem for us is not so much saying yes to such a proposal from the giver of life but one of coming to grips with how such a good fortune could be possible. The first Christians called this divine election the "gospel," that is, the "good news." Unfortunately, it is still news for many thousands to this very day. What a wonderful surprise awaits those who seek out the designs of God.

Being Transformed

The SCC is uniquely and ideally suited to express the fullness of the priesthood of Jesus because it requires involvement of one's total person in the recognition of one's identity as the beloved of God. Becoming a spouse is not a matter of putting on a superficial badge or wearing a ring. Rather, it requires a radical reorientation of one's person to the voice of the beloved. An espousal relationship is the summit of personal expression and commitment.

SCC is the setting that best allows an individual to awaken to the touch of the divine suitor, much like the fabled sleeping beauty awakened to the touch of the relentlessly faithful prince. A response to a divine marriage proposal is not possible through some abstract mental or emotional process. All of creation awaits the "I do" response from each of us to the divine proposal before the whole universe breaks out in festivities.

When you come together as SCC, your response is taking

form. In your gathering the Spirit of Christ is present to nurture your espousal "yes." The depth of your yes transforms you inwardly. Experience of this inward transformation is your evidence to the call that first began as an act of faith. What was hidden as a priceless treasure is now brought into view for you. At the same time you are transfigured outwardly by radiating in your features what is occurring within, thus attracting others to the new world.

The exercise of priesthood by members of SCC is important because as we are more and more open to a divine espousal relationship, we become more and more open to each other. Our yes to God is not said in a secret or theoretical manner but in the context of our relationship to others. Accepting God's proposal necessarily brings us into dialogue with one another because there are not many gods but one living God who can be all things to all persons in such a way as to preserve the uniqueness of each. The reality of our yes to God must pass the acid test of our relationship to the neighbor, who is called to the same divine espousal relationship. We are in the process of reversing the murderous deceit of Cain which was the consequence of Adam and Eve's decision to shut God out of human dialogue.

Tabor Experience in Us

You have been meeting with your SCC for a period of time during which some real sharing has occurred. It is not uncommon to hear remarks from time to time such as: "It is good for us to be here." Recall that these were the same words uttered by Peter at the gathering on Mt. Tabor. The person speaking is reflecting a sense of enrichment in his or her life as a result of the gatherings. This experience provides evidence that a transforming action of grace is bringing us closer to one another while at the same time we are each being drawn closer in a unique espousal relationship with our divine suitor. A member finds within a deep sense of peace, and consciously or unconsciously radiates (transfigures) it wherever he or she goes. The peace radiated attracts others like birds to a safe shelter.

Thus, in a small way the transformation that has occurred within a person has been transfigured (made visible) in order to draw others into the loving, divine dialogue. Genuine love cannot be concealed. Look into a person's eyes, which are the windows of his or her soul (Luke 11:34). Some eyes are cold, distant, expressionless, and dead. Looking into the face of someone whose life is shallow because of seeking power or the selfish pleasure of the moment is like looking into the expressionless face of a cow. In contrast, the faces of others not so addicted are lively and radiant, revealing a living transformation occurring within.

Note the radiant joy in the face of a well loved child. Many lose this spark from heaven because they do not know how to fan into flame what God has already begun the moment God calls them into being. It is not that God breaks off the dialogue, but people become satisfied with the superficial. Healing comes from seeking to re-establish the human-divine dialogue. This otherwise hidden human-divine espousal dialogue, when made visible, is called transfiguration; it is the bestowing of a visible image (i.e., "figure") on an unseen world within. This is the first evidence of the world that is coming.

Worship as Essence of SCC

In this chapter our focus is on the SCC as a worshipping community. It was necessary to first reflect on the gathering of the first SCC on Mt. Tabor to gain an understanding of priesthood and worship. We have so far described a radically new understanding of worship that was introduced by Jesus. Such understanding is critical to the life of SCC. Membership in SCC requires a tremendous commitment of self to worship as a way of life that seeks to bring the good news of the gospel (i.e., one's election as the beloved of God) to oneself and therefore to the world. Worship consisting in our growing acceptance of who we are constitutes the very essence of the life of SCC.

It would be a great mistake to try to simply replicate in SCC worship as it is expressed in large groups. Genuine worship (that is, transformation brought about by divine-human dialogue) must begin at the personal level. Gatherings in public settings, such as in large groups on Sundays, must be seen as the extension of a personal commitment to a life of worship, as explained above. This is not a criticism of those who have always viewed worship as something owed to God, or as a way of giving thanksgiving for favors received, or as a means for making restitution for sins to gain future blessings, or, perhaps, to set good example for children. SCC requires a much deeper understanding of worship.

When worship is properly understood, the need for small community is perfectly obvious. In a large group it is very easy to fall into the practice of all show and no substance. To be a worshipping (i.e. priestly) community it is necessary for people to constantly strive toward consciousness of a divine espousal relationship, like an Olympic athlete straining for the gold medal. After 2000 years, the Christian world is still far from being able to grasp God's intentions in our behalf.

In a small community the struggle is easier because progress is more discernable. An ongoing membership in SCC is the best guarantee that you will make progress in the struggle to achieve the lofty identity God has conferred upon you. However, the SCC that is based on the ancient notion of worship—"paying to God what is due"—will not stand the test of time. If your SCC survives, it is virtually certain that you will grow to know who you are. Your SCC makes sense only in terms of providing an arena to deal with the divinely revealed fact that you are the beloved. The struggle to grasp this divine election is the substance that gives meaning to Christian worship.

Offering Hospitality

We need to find practical ways of bringing out among members of our SCC a greater awareness that our gatherings are first and foremost an action of worship, that is, an effort to say yes to our divine election as beloved.

Perhaps the best way to foster a sense of being a worshipping community is to do what Peter did on Mt. Tabor. His immediate response to his experience was to offer hospitality in the form of setting up tents for the guests. From this we learn that the first requirement of worship is to treat people as the beloved of God because how otherwise would they know? Words are empty unless followed by action.

The person(s) hosting the meeting should set the tone by treating members as honored guests. Greet each person by name, make each feel welcomed, and offer sincere compliments whenever possible. Above all, make your guests thoroughly comfortable. Worship does not require physical discomfort. Some meetings last three to four hours during which a hard chair can become very hard indeed. Also, resist any inclination to show favoritism. Make all equally welcome, from the most distinguished visitor to the least, mindful that each is equally called by the divine spouse who alone sees the heart of each.

Treating your guests well means seating them so that everyone can see and hear. If people choose to stay in the background and be spectators, it must be by their choice not yours. Be aware, also, of the temperature in the room. If the meeting place is too hot or cold it shows a lack of consideration on the part of the host(ess). If people want to do penance, let them do it on their own, in their own homes. However, economic necessity is another issue. The point here is that an atmosphere of worship does not require physical discomfort. A good host will use every means available to make guests welcome and comfortable.

Form of Worship

Normally, the person hosting the meeting is also the leader of worship. A warm welcome is in itself the beginning of worship. The continuation of worship ought to be in the form of sharing whatever is of concern to each SCC member. Worship should then naturally move to its high point in the form of sharing sacred Scripture. Each of us are making the same faith journey, using the wisdom accumulated in Scripture left to us by hundreds and thousands of people who have journeyed before us.

To relate to the parish at large, it makes sense to use readings that will be used in the Sunday liturgy. The leader should select readers and prepare discussion questions in advance. As the meeting progresses, the discussion of the readings should shift from an academic exercise to a personal sharing of what the readings mean.

Scripture serves as a compass for our individual faith journeys. Most have at least some vague notion of what it means to be God's beloved. By sharing one's vision of the divine courtship in the context of Scripture, other members of the community are able to better understand their own journey.

Many, unfortunately, are bogged down because they have no spiritual self-image. They choose to focus on what they "do" as a fire-fighter, lawyer, programmer, plumber, or whatever. When a person speaks of himself or herself as a "recovering" architect or doctor, they are referring to their discovery that they are persons above and beyond their functional roles in society.

Still others must struggle with a poor, sometimes negative self-image and must work themselves free of useless baggage they have dragged along with them for years. The heaviest bag of all is a feeling they are helpless. SCC is a warm, receptive environment where each of us find opportunity to peel away the rubbish and finally uncover the treasure of being the beloved of God.

Sharing should naturally move toward prayer. In essence,

prayer is a lifting of our gaze to the Tabor mountain top toward which we are journeying. Prayer is firmly based on the clear awareness of where a person is and reaches out to the next step toward an espousal relationship with God. Genuine prayer will also reflect our changing relationships with one another because an espousal relationship to the one living God has profound implications for our other relationships.

Finally, SCC worship should move from the kind of prayer that seeks a better vision of the world to come, to looking at where we have been. The journey has been long, but we continue to press ahead with a heart overwhelmed with thanks ("eucharist" comes from the Greek word for thanks). All worship is crystallized in an ecstatic sense of thanksgiving. We are like people lost for days in a dark cave emerging into the sunlight for the first time. The brilliant good fortune of being the elect of God is both ecstasy and agony as we come to consciousness of our dignity. We maintain our center of control in the form of an ever-increasing sense of thanksgiving. This experience of thanksgiving is an experience of communion not only with God, but also with our neighbor, that is, other members of our SCC, each of whom is being called to communion with God.

Worship with Substance

While we celebrate thanksgiving in our SCC for what God is doing for each of us, we also gather publicly in a more or less large group on Sunday in a eucharistic (thanksgiving) feast as a way of manifesting that what God is doing in our SCC, God is doing for the whole world.

For worship to be complete, it must not be left in the realm of the symbolic but must be translated into our lives in concrete, practical ways. For this reason it is helpful to end your SCC meeting by sharing a meal together as a way of giving thanks for each other. Love of God is inseparable from love of neighbor, which should be evident from the entire tone of this chapter. A meal is an opportunity for all to give, and at the same time to experience, how rewarding it is when all generously contribute. How much more flavor there is in food that is shared with friends!

Thus, worship encompasses the whole of the SCC gathering, from the initial preparations, to the greeting upon arrival, to Scripture discussion, to sharing, prayer, thanksgiving, and a communal meal. Some may have had a more restrictive notion of worship and prayer. Be aware that anything put under a microscope is unrecognizable until one draws back to regain the vision of an unaided eye. In entering into SCC, it is like looking at worship through a microscope where interconnections are made visible. This does not detract from familiar worship performed in large buildings but gives meaning and understanding to it. Worship must not be just for show but must have substance. Otherwise, our worship would be a mockery of the nuptial proposal God has made through Jesus.

As mentioned previously, the essence of worship is increasingly accepting one's dignity as the beloved of God. Comprehension of this reality is beyond language's capacity to express or the imagination's ability to conceive. Worship, by definition, is our effort to come to grips with an espousal relationship with a divine suitor.

To achieve this goal, it is helpful from time to time to select a theme for the worship in your SCC. The theme may, for example, reflect the liturgical year of the whole church: Lent, Holy Week, Easter, Pentecost, Advent, Christmas. Identifying your SCC worship with the worship of the universal church helps to make members of your SCC aware that the whole world is engaged in a cosmic struggle to define the divine-human espousal relationship revealed on Mt. Tabor. Saint Paul, reflecting on this, compares the labor of all creation to bring forth the beloved, to the struggle of a mother who in painful labor anxiously waits to see and hold the new life soon to emerge (Romans 8:22).

Themes for worship may also be selected according to the particular interest or needs of your SCC. The following are two examples of how to conduct your SCC meeting using the themes of "desert" and "word."

DESERT THEME

Introduction
(Read this at the beginning of the meeting.)

The theme for our worship today is the desert. All major religions in the world today, for example, Hinduism, Buddhism, Islam, Judaism, and Christianity, originated in a desert or isolated place. If we are to grasp the meaning of our religion, we, too, must go into the desert from which it came.

The desert is a desolate place; it numbs the senses and imagination; it surrounds one with an overpowering aloneness. Let us pause now and listen to the sounds of the desert. (Pause for five minutes in complete silence. Then read the following selections from Scripture.)

Reading 1 The Israelites wander for forty years in the desert (Genesis 16: 1-4, 3-35).

Reading 2 John the Baptist preaches in the desert and lives on locust and honey (Matthew 3:1-6).

Reading 3 Jesus spends forty days and forty nights in the desert (Matthew 4:1-4).

Questions for Discussion
1. Desert is the soul of religion. What is the significance of this?

2. What effects did their 40-year desert experience have on the Israelites?

3. Consider the importance of the desert for John the Bap-

tist and Jesus. Did it serve as an escape? From what? To what? Explain.

Questions for Personal Sharing

1. Have you had a desert experience in your life? Explain.
2. How can you bring the desert into your busy world?
3. Do people distract you from God? What does the desert experience really mean to you?

Prayer

(Read the following and then share personal prayer in the spirit of John the Baptist.)

John the Baptist said, "I am a voice crying in the desert preparing the way of the Lord. Every valley will be filled and every mountain brought low."

John both announces and invites us to enter a new relationship with God that far exceeds any hitherto known. By comparison, all previous images of God are as a barren desert. The new world that is dawning exceeds the deepest valleys of our human desires and the highest mountains of our imagination. What has been known hitherto is but of shadow of what is at hand.

Celebration

(When the shared prayer is completed, quietly move on to a shared meal.)

The meal of celebration may reflect the desert theme. We do not suggest that you serve locust in imitation of John the Baptist, but honey would be appropriate. The Israelites ate manna. Perhaps something that symbolizes manna can be served. A very dry wine would be appropriate. One or two dishes that bring out the theme would be sufficient.

Word Theme

(Read the following introduction at the beginning of the meeting.)

In ancient times breath and life were identical notions. The unscientific people of 2000 years ago observed that when breath left the body so did life. Furthermore, they observed that no word could be uttered without breath. It seemed obvious to them, therefore, that a person's word and life were inseparable. Thus, if people broke their word, they at the same time ended their life. Accordingly, it was expected that people would be executed or would freely take their own life because life had no further meaning.

It is within this context that Christianity was conceived. Jesus is described as the "Word made flesh." In effect this means putting one's own neck where one's mouth is. Today words are so plentiful and cheap that word pollution is among the worst pollutants of our environment. Human communication has virtually ended. SCC, among other things, is an attempt to restore human communication. The flood of words coming from television, radio, and the printed page has ironically produced something of a silence because meaning has been virtually drained from words. Words today are used to manipulate, not to communicate.

In contrast, words in ancient times meant more than life itself. The name given a person was meant to identify the very essence of that person. In keeping with this perspective, the first Christians sought to identify the meaning of Jesus, his life, words and works, with one word. The word that was chosen was "Christ." This is the Greek word for "anointed" with the connotation of "beloved." Christ is not the last name of Jesus but a name that identifies his mission and purpose. His first followers were soon identified as the "beloved ones."

Names in ancient times were understood as a revelation of identity.

Reading 1 Zachary insists on the name John (Luke 1:57-79).
Reading 2 Mary is told she will have a son who is to be named Jesus (Luke 1:28-33).

Reading 3 The name of Simon is changed to Peter, signifying rock (John 1:40-42; Matthew 16:13-18).

Questions for Discussion

1. Because of his disbelief, Zachary was unable to speak until the circumcision of John. What does this say about the connection between faith and word?

2. Mary believed the word of God and God became flesh. What does this say about the connection between flesh and God? Between our own word and our own flesh?

3. Peter believed the word and was immediately designated as "rock." What is the connection between our belief in SCC and this response of Christ?

Questions for Personal Sharing

Consciously or unconsciously, our own lives are being expressed in one word. For example, "freedom" aptly expresses the life and values of Martin Luther King. It takes considerable reflection, but each of us probably can summarize our lives in one word.

Each member of the SCC should write down the word that expresses who he or she is. Now write a word that expresses the identity of each person present. The words selected must be complimentary, not critical or judgmental. The leader should first share his or her own word and then listen while each member reveals the word selected for the leader's life. Then go around the room repeating the process so that all will have an experience of the power of the word made flesh. Then share these questions.

1. Some are easier to identify with one word than others. Why?

2. What does this worship focused on the "word" mean in your life?

3. What word made flesh in your life do you hope will remain when you are gone?

Prayer

The entire Song of Songs in the Old Testament is in the form of words from the divine bridegroom to his beloved. Each member of the SCC should select a meaningful passage and read it as an introduction to shared prayer.

Celebration and Thanksgiving

The leader can set the tone for the meal by buying in advance some small, inexpensive item for each member that "expresses" each person, for example, a dove for a person who is a peace maker, a candle for one who contributes remarkable insights, a pen for one gifted in writing, and so forth. Gift wrap the items and place them at each person's place at the table. Members may then each in turn open their gifts. This gesture of gift-giving symbolizes the unique "gift" each person is to the community. The conversation that follows during the meal will put a final sparkle on the worship experience.

Conclusion

People who compartmentalize life into work, family, Sunday worship, leisure time, and the like will find this chapter very difficult to understand. No apology is in order. Understanding priesthood, that is, worship, in the new world inaugurated by Jesus requires a quantum leap in awareness. We are not talking about simply rearranging the furniture. If SCC becomes just another activity to be fitted in, rather than that which gives meaning to everything we do, or if we are unable to perceive life as a seamless garment, our comprehension of worship, the heartbeat of SCC, will be impossible. SCC is, after all, not an end in itself but a means for putting people in touch with the living God. After such an encounter, as at Mt. Tabor, a person will never be the same again.

Volumes could be written on the meaning of Christian worship. In essence, worship is the unfolding of a love story in which we are surrounded by the universe of God's love. We are ever so slow to awaken to the cosmic drama in which we play the lead role. Our SCC serves as our wake-up call.

Though much could be written, enough has been said to give you some perspective on worship as the heartbeat of your SCC. In our next chapter we will shift from the heart to the head. Your SCC has a prophetic role that you share with Christ.

Before we begin looking at the prophetic dimensions of SCCs, take a look back at this chapter and review the salient issues. It would not be surprising if this chapter raised more questions than answers in your mind. As you delve more deeply into the meaning and practice of worship, what at first appeared quite natural and simple takes on much more complexity. Perhaps a series of questions and answers followed by some discussion questions for your SCC will be helpful in digesting the content of this chapter.

QUESTIONS AND ANSWERS

Q. In the Bible Jesus is projected as the son of God, not the spouse of God. Which is it?

A. There is no gender in God. Father and son are not meant to assert gender but are anthropomorphic words. We use relational words such as father and son because of the limitations of our language. Jesus was also constrained by human language, and he therefore spoke only in parables about God and us. His favorite parable for expressing our relationship with God is that of a marriage feast, an espousal relationship. He could not have spoken so eloquently of that relationship had he himself not experienced it.

In our sophisticated world, which advancement in social sciences has introduced, a more useful image for our relationship to God is "my other self." This is another way of expressing an espousal relationship. As a result of years of dialogue, spouses in a marriage become the other self to each other. "God as my other self" expresses the notion that God has sought dialogue with me since time began and loves me far more than I could ever love myself. Our gradual acceptance of this gratuitous relationship on the part of God is bringing us to life. The more we say yes to God's proposal, the more we reflect God. Thus, God is my other self, not in terms of nature but in terms of God's gratuitous love on my behalf.

Q. Isn't the espousal relationship as reflected on Mt. Tabor for Christ alone?

A. No. Christ is the new Adam, the originator of the new human race. This means that Christ is the prototype of our relationship with God. What God has done in Christ, God is doing for each of us who respond yes to God's proposal. This is the essence of the gospel, the "God-spell," or the good news, proclaimed by Christ to the world. This truth is proclaimed again and again as persons accept the divine proposal throughout history, thereby freely choosing to join the new human race because the race of the old Adam is passing away.

Q. How can we be sure that we are not deluding ourselves in pursuing such a mind-exploding proposition as an espousal relationship with God?

A. An espousal relationship with God is the unique contribution of Christ to the evolution of religion in history. How do we prove the truth of this espousal election? Your question touches on the greatest riddle of history. Saint Paul tells us we will have our proof, but only after we believe. Faith comes first and proof of the object of faith follows (Hebrews 11:1).

As you began to be transformed by your unique relationship with God, other members of your SCC will see the effects in your relationship to them. In this way a witness to the truth is given. All enjoy the loving warmth that is generated, but this does not mean other members have faith. They may be living off the faith of just one member. Even though they witness the emerging espousal relationship of one member, they may be unwilling to believe the reality of it. The apostles lived off the faith of Jesus until he was taken away. Only then did they begin to develop their own faith. If our election is a delusion, then Christ and 2000 years of Christian faith constitute the world's cruelest scam.

Q. Worship in this chapter is viewed as a way of life rather than as an activity. Are there stages in worship similar to stages in life?

A. Yes. Young people in SCC are struggling with their own identity. They tend to do a lot of sifting, thus they often quietly listen at SCC gatherings and spend a lot of time sorting out their feelings, ideas, and events.

Middle-aged members have arrived at a fairly well-formed identity and are anxious to generate a multitude of ideas and activities that will serve to enhance their vision of what the world should be to reflect the gospel and how to bring about the changes needed in the world.

For older people, worship is an activity of integration in which they began to view their whole life as a dialogue with a loving God that began at the moment of birth. At this stage, there is a tendency to look back over life and to feel that it was all worthwhile and to look forward to the divine nuptials toward which their lives are directed. Persons in this last stage of worship are ideal leaders of worship in SCC. They have less to say, but when speaking do so from the heart.

Q. Isn't a priest the only one that can lead worship and change bread and wine into the body and blood of Christ?

A. The church with all of its members is by definition a worshipping community. The worship by an ordained priest does not detract from the dynamic worship that occurs in a small community. The priest has power to lead only from the church itself, not from his own wish. When he speaks for the church, he can transform bread and wine into the body and blood of Christ. He can do this because Christ is already present where two or more gather in his name.

When your SCC comes together, Christ is always really and truly there, not as a guest but as the host of the meeting. He is inviting you into dialogue with himself and with one another as the way to enter espousal dialogue with God. All of this effort constitutes true worship. An ordained priest in current practice simply carries the notion of worship to a larger gathering, which, far from detracting, is intended to support worship at the SCC level.

Q. Should we allow a person from another religion to participate in our SCC worship?

A. Remember that the divine romance is going on in every heart. It is not for us to define or set limits. Christianity is the world's only espousal religion, and therefore all Christians should be comfortable in SCC where the human-divine dialogue is fostered. Islam and Judaism are tribal religions. Both accept Christ as an outstanding member of their religious tribe and therefore could benefit from dialogue with Christ in SCC.

Hindus and Buddhists view the path to God as a process that by necessity leads to the elimination of the notion of "person," or individual, in an attempt to identify with the vital force of life itself. Consequently, dialogue is impossible because the human part of the human-divine dialogue is eliminated.

Hindus and Buddhists are probably not interested in coming to SCC where dialogue is of the very essence. All, however, should be welcomed as a part of SCC because the love generated in SCC can only spark an interest in dialogue in a heart long caught up in a disciplined silence. The silence characteristic of Eastern religions such as Hinduism and Buddhism can in turn influence Christians to a deeper level of dialogue.

Q. Can you be more specific about the "transformation or transfiguration" effect of worship?

A. When two people fall in love, others often poke fun because of the effect love has on them. Lovers have a new bounce in their step, joy in their voice, and a glow on their faces, especially, the eyes. Human love is but a pale reflection, like a spark before a brilliant sun, of the unfolding love between the beloved and the divine suitor. If transfiguration is not occurring in a person's life, the chances are the person has intellectualized religion too much with too little expression in the form of dialogue-centered worship.

Q. Should each person in SCC have opportunity to lead in worship?

A. Ideally, yes. As the gathering of the SCC moves from home to home, it is appropriate that the host lead in worship because the host is in the position of inviting guests (members of the SCC). A leader in worship (priest) is by definition an inviter, drawing others deeper into dialogue as a way to God.

Members should not, however, be forced or pressured to lead in worship. Furthermore, the one leading must have the implicit or explicit delegation of the members because the leader is attempting to express the identity of the community as a whole. Members must feel some investment in the leader to make the worship both real and effective in evolving their own identity as beloved of God, as well as the identity of the total gathering.

Q. I have always thought of worship as paying my debt to God. Isn't too much emphasis being placed on the human dimension of SCC?

A. Parents would not even think of writing up an itemized invoice for services rendered for 18 years or more and then send it to a child. Love demands response not payment. So, too, the intimate divine-human espousal proposition revealed by Christ as the only worthy image of God, demands response, not debt payment. Reverence for God is based not on respectful-but-distant fear but on grateful-but-intimate love in response.

The SCC is formed, not because God needs it, but as the most ideal environment to discover and foster our espousal relationship with God, to insure through dialogue with real people that one does not pursue a delusion, and to have people present to receive the healing overflow of thanks and love as members open up to the divine proposition.

Q. How do devotions such as those to the Blessed Mother, Sacred Heart, Saint Francis, and others fit into SCC?

A. Devotions are intended primarily to serve individual piety. Any devotional practice that is helpful to an individual should be encouraged. SCC is not private in that sense. It is not focused on private devotion but is an effort to make the church present in the modern world. Unlike devotions that focus on individual piety, the SCC serves as a witness to the total community of the presence of Christ in history, in our time and place.

As we gather increasingly in the spirit of Christ, putting away our own shortsighted blindness, Christ becomes more and more visible to us and through us to the world. If the world goes on its way ignoring the church building, however beautifully constructed, people of the world will sit up and take notice if a small community of believers makes the risen Christ visible in their midst.

QUESTIONS FOR REVIEW AND DISCUSSION

1. What is the difference between transformation and transfiguration? How can we recognize it in people around us?

2. How was worship understood before the time of Moses? What new dimension did Moses add? What further dimension did Christ add?

3. Espousal relationship must be between equals. How then can we speak of an espousal relationship between ourselves and God?

4. In what ways are Sunday worship at the parish and worship in your SCC related? Why are both necessary?

5. All worship basically is an experience of thanksgiving. Explain.

6. For Christians, worship goes beyond rituals, prayers, and devotions. What does this mean? How does worship touch our daily lives?

7. How does an espousal relationship with God affect our relationship with each other?

8. Why is the experience of peace a hallmark of true worship?

9. Is SCC needed in the Christian perception of worship? Why?

10. In what ways does the person hosting SCC meeting reflect what a leader in Christian worship should be?

Chapter 5

That They All May Be One

"That they all may be one even as you, Father, are in me and I in you; that they also may be one in us that the world may believe that you sent me. And the glory that you have given me, I have given to them, that they may be one, even as we are one: I in them and you in me; that they may be perfected in unity, and that the world may know that you sent me, and that you loved them even as you loved me" (John 17:20-23).

In this prayer, Jesus reveals an espousal person-to-person relationship with God. He introduces a new image of God far surpassing the vital and tribal images hitherto known in religious history. Henceforth the espousal is the only fully adequate image worthy of God for humankind. Rightly, Jesus is heralded as the greatest prophet of all times. In his prayer he reveals the ultimate conceptualization of the divine-human relationship, one that surpasses all previous images as day surpasses the night in brilliance. Little, if anything, can be added to the eloquence of this prayer wherein Jesus prays that all may be one as he and God are one, that all may be perfected in unity. Then all the world will know Jesus is from God and that God loves each, even as God loves Jesus.

In the previous chapter we said that Jesus introduced a new priesthood consisting of an invitation to us to accept our call to be the beloved of God. Our response to that invitation is the only true worship worthy of God. Worship henceforth can come only from hearts that are at the same time transformed by acceptance of the divine proposal. Our decision is genuine worship because our yes is the only thing in the whole universe that is beyond God's reach. Our personal acceptance of a divine espousal relationship adds something radically new to God wherein God is supremely glorified, thus fulfilling the purpose of the priesthood Jesus initiates. In this chapter our thoughts will be directed toward Jesus as prophet and the prophetic role of your SCC, because your SCC is the extension of the presence of Jesus in our time and place.

It is an olympian task to understand the priesthood of your SCC in the context of the Mt. Tabor experience, as presented in the last chapter. The mountain of understanding you are about to climb in this chapter will present an even greater challenge for your SCC. Once again, our purpose is to act as your guide until you are able to get your bearing about what it means for your SCC to serve in a prophetic role.

Meaning of "Prophet"

First, it is of the greatest importance to understand that, contrary to popular belief, prophecy does not mean foretelling the future. The essence of prophecy is pointing to what God is doing here and now. By doing this, the prophet facilitates the response of human beings to the creative, healing action of God. The God of Jesus is not a distant ruler waiting to pass judgment on our every action but a living God eminently present and ready to pour life into the heart of the believer. An effective prophet is one who enables God to quicken our life as we are drawn ever nearer to the living God, until we are ready for the final heart exploding face-to-face encounter with our betrothed. A person who has long been in a darkened cave cannot immediately walk out into the bright sunlight. So, too, with each of us, it is only after many small increases to the intensity of our life that we will be able to stand before the very source of life.

Evil was personified in ancient times as deceit (darkness) in the form of the devil Lucifer ("bearer of light"). Creating darkness and deceit is the antithesis of prophecy. One who practices deceit increases the darkness, thus frustrating the designs of God. On the other hand, Jesus, the true prophet, is fittingly presented in John's gospel as the true light shining in the darkness to light the path of every person.

The one brilliant truth prophetically revealed by Jesus is that God has been from the very beginning our relentless suitor who has been unwilling to take no for an answer. In regard to this truth, we still dwell in darkness both within ourselves and in the world around us. We often find it easier to believe lies than the truth, especially when the truth has so many mind-numbing implications.

Your SCC picks up the spark from Christ who is in your midst. Your prophetic role is to gently fan that spark through growth in loving dialogue until it bursts into flame and provides light for all to see what God is doing here and now. Thus, the resulting unity in your SCC is a light in the darkened world revealing God's uniting action. Your experience of communion constitutes proof to yourselves, as well as to the world, that Jesus is indeed from God and continues to live in and through your SCC.

It should be clear from this discussion that prophecy and unity are two sides of the same coin. If your SCC achieves a greater measure of unity, which is in no way based upon physical, economic, mental, psychological, or spiritual force, then it can only be the action of God, because the ultimate source of unity is the divine-human espousal relationship. Furthermore, the unity that arises within your SCC cannot be forced because this would require manipulation and deceit. True unity must arise from one or more individuals discovering and accepting a more intimate divine espousal relationship. The resulting transformation within the person is then reflected in actions characteristic of a person in love, thus giving evidence (witness) to others concerning the designs God has upon all of us. Furthermore, your SCC as a whole enjoys a greater sense of community when one of its members accepts at a new depth his or her calling as God's beloved.

Role of the Individual

You may have never thought of yourself as a prophet. You may find it easier to view global leaders who bring about a remarkable measure of unity as prophets. The first one that comes to mind is Pope John XXIII who sparked a remarkable level of global unity during the short time he was pope. The world was briefly united in an experience of mourning at the death of president John F. Kennedy who had raised the hope for a better world. During the 1960s, many people identified with the ringing call for freedom voiced by Martin Luther King, Jr. Such individuals are like flashes of lightening in the night sky pointing to the deep yearning we all feel for an ultimate unity.

Unfortunately, unity does not come on a global scale, but only on a personal level. Global unity is the result, not the cause, of unity at the personal level. Thus, it is very appropriate to think of yourself as a prophet. Whenever you become a catalyst for a deeper unity in your SCC, home, neighborhood, place of work, or worship, you exercise a prophetic role. You are revealing what God is doing for the entire human race.

It is very difficult for an isolated individual to get a sense of being prophetic. Membership in SCC serves to make unity at a personal level more visible, and accordingly your prophetic calling becomes more obvious. It is only by understanding unity at the personal level in your SCC that unity can be understood and achieved at the parish, regional, national, and global level.

Becoming a prophet, however, is not an easy road to travel. If the prayer of Jesus for unity is to be fulfilled through our accepting the divine proposal of espousal relationship, then it will be realized only through the long, laborious efforts of opening our hearts to the divine call and, as a consequence, to one another. Your SCC is the workshop for that understanding. Prophecy flows from your understanding of God's designs. From your prophecy others will be drawn toward understanding. The resulting unity will be a sign to all that Jesus who sparks your prophetic mission is indeed from God.

God as the Source of Unity

It should now be evident that the human race cannot be treated like a herd of animals united by the strongest beast, but must seek unity from and in God. Looked at from another viewpoint, when the human race finally achieves the unity it so deeply craves, God will be fully revealed.

This statement is so obvious it's almost simplistic. Strangely, however, what appears simple, is sometimes very complex. What could be easier than for your SCC, to sit back and enjoy the level of unity you have achieved? Who in the world could blame you for resting on your laurels and closing your eyes to the discord in the world that surrounds you? Don't be misled. Each member of your SCC must strive mightily toward an understanding of each other in order to find ever deeper levels of oneness, a oneness that the world cannot give. It can come only from God because a new level of unity requires a deeper revelation of God. The new revelation is, in essence, a proclamation to the world of God's abiding presence among us.

Your SCC is small precisely so that unity will go beyond a

family or tribe to a deeper personal level. Paul is reflecting on this deeper level of union when he points out that there will be neither Jew or Gentile, male or female, bond or free (Galatians 3:28). This involves getting your own life together as an individual, and the people in your SCC act as catalysts to help you to deal with yourself at ever deeper levels. When you do so you bring a greater unity to your SCC as a whole.

Experiencing unity in your SCC is not enough. If growing unity in the world is in fact the ongoing revelation of God, it is most important that you grow in your understanding of unity as the very basis for knowing God. Furthermore, your SCC must continually strive for greater understanding of all the dimensions of unity in order to give an account to those attracted as well as to those threatened by the influence you generate. Unity is like a many-faceted gem that reveals an endless spectacle of beauty as it is viewed from different vantage points. So, too, the unity in your SCC must be viewed from many perspectives to gain a deeper appreciation of it.

For this reason, it is useful to look at the prophetic unity in your SCC from a variety of perspectives, namely: historical, moral, theological, sacramental, political and teleological. Remember, you are not the first nor the last to labor for a more visible presence of God in and through the level of oneness you experience in SCC. Presenting a variety of perspectives on unity in your SCC will make the task of pursuing union with God through communion with each other easier.

Historical Perspective

SCC has ancient roots. Twelve hundred years before Christ the Israelites were scattered, enslaved, and destined for extermination in the land of Egypt. God entered history as a uniting, freeing, and saving influence for the tribe of Israel through the hand and voice of Moses. The people of Israel were very slow to recognize the presence of Yahweh in their midst, and consequently needed forty years of wandering aimlessly in the desert of Sinai to become one tribe drawn together by Yahweh, whom they grew to perceive as their divine chieftain.

During this time, the tribe of Israel adopted ten commandments that were to serve as the basis of unity among themselves and with God. Observance of these laws produced tribal unity pleasing to Yahweh. Finally, at the moment of entering into the promised land, all the Israelites, composed of twelve separate tribes descended from the twelve sons of Jacob, were called together around an altar built for Yahweh consisting of twelve stones. Worship was offered with the admonition that, even though the twelve tribes were about to settle in different areas of the promised land, Yahweh would remain the chieftain that bound them all together. Observance of the ten commandments was to serve as the barometer of their fidelity to one another and to God.

It is worthy of note here that the Israelites thought of themselves as the chosen people or tribe because they were the first in history to think of God, not in the traditional formless image of being identical to life, but as one you could talk to and interact with. Since the only social structure known to Semitic peoples 3000 to 4000 years ago was tribal, God was naturally perceived to be the tribal chief, which was the position of highest honor. The Israelites then perceived themselves to be a chosen tribe because the dignity of a tribe is derived from its chief. Arab countries today still operate on a tribal basis. The leader is believed to embody the whole tribe. What is important is that the image of God was raised out of the eternal rhythm of nature to a tribal image. God was involved in history. Jesus later elevated the image of God beyond tribal to a personal level. Each person is chosen as beloved of Yahweh.

The Old Testament gives an account of the long struggle toward maintaining tribal unity, recording failure more often than success. Prophets, needed because there was no hierarchy to be spokesperson for the divine chief of the tribe, were raised up time and again to point to observance of the law as the way to obtain the uniting action of Yahweh. After repeated failures, the people finally rebelled against Yahweh's exercise of invisible leadership through prophets and demanded a very visible king with hierarchy and laws like all the other nations around them had. They could thus remove any doubt as to what God expected of the people. Samuel, the leading prophet at the time, finally yielded to their demands, warning them that dire consequences would follow their losing touch with Yahweh their true tribal chief. He anointed Saul as the first king of Israel.

Saul's kingship was shortlived because he chose a path of violence and superstition as a means of uniting his people. This resulted in his rejection by the prophet Samuel and the anointing of David as the new king of Israel. David, in contrast to Saul, recognized his partnership with Yahweh and, consequently, succeeded in uniting all the people of Israel. Henceforth, David became the symbol of unity to the people of Israel. Because unity is the hallmark of God's presence, the prophets concluded that a coming messiah must be a descendant of David to bring unity to the entire world. Little did the prophets realize the union that the Messiah would proclaim would go far beyond the tribal/political concept of unity achieved by King David. Jesus revealed that God is identical with the source of unity.

As time went on, the people of Israel became so presumptuous of the tribal unity provided through Yahweh, that they recklessly defied the military power of neighboring states. Irritated, the King of Babylon, in 587 B.C., sent his army to devastate the land of Israel, destroy the temple of Yahweh in Jerusalem, and bring the tribe of Juda (the Jews), defenders of the temple, as slaves to Babylon.

With the downfall of the king of Israel, the leadership of prophets once again rose to prominence. Under the influence of prophets, the enslaved Jews decided to preserve their allegiance to Yahweh by gathering weekly in small groups of about ten men (women and children at this time were considered inferior) to share their faith. This institution became known as a "synagogue" (Hebrew, for "assembly").

Invention of this innovative practice enabled Judaism to eventually spread throughout the world and it endures to the present day. After forty-nine years of captivity in Babylon, the Jews were allowed to return to their own land. But Judaism had profoundly changed through the influence of the synagogue so that most Jews felt no need of returning to the land of Israel. They felt that they could live out their fidelity to Yahweh anywhere through their involvement in a synagogue. For the first time the notion of being a chosen tribe was not restricted to the land of Palestine but was thought of as a worldwide phenomenon whereby Jews were united less by blood than through the bonds of religion or faith in a coming messiah who would bring the unity King David once brought to the people of Israel.

When Jesus came on the scene he addressed himself, not to the temple hierarchy in Jerusalem, but primarily to the small local synagogues. His remark, in which he said where even two (in contrast to about ten in a synagogue) come together in his name, he is in their midst (Matthew 12:20), reflected his focus on the institution of the synagogue. Jesus added a new prophetic dimension by pointing out that henceforth it is not for men only. In the new "synagogue," emphasis would be on each person, a reality beyond being male or female, Jew or Gentile, slave or free, because all would be as one with God (Galatians 3:28).

Thus, historically, SCCs are directly related to the synagogue. For many years the Jewish and Christian communities were identical because most early converts were Jews who continued to gather weekly in small communities and read the letters of the apostles along with the writings of the ancient prophets. The first great crisis that arose in the church centered around the issue of whether Christianity was just another sect of Judaism or a radically new element. The apostles resolved the conflict by declaring that a radically new element had been introduced by Christ wherein the Gentile is to be regarded as equal to the Jew because both are persons. Henceforth, Yahweh, the tribal chieftain of the Israelites, is to be known as the God of the individual, i.e., Christ. This is the God who is the source of unity for all humankind.

This is a highly simplified, thumbnail sketch of 4000 years of religious history. If your SCC is to serve effectively in a prophetic capacity, it is important that at least this much of your roots be known. Only by entering into the hard work of dialogue within your SCC will you gain an adequate idea of how your ancestors have struggled with the presence of God in human history. A historical perspective is needed in your endeavor to form SCC so that you can appreciate how it is a continuation of the work of countless other people who have labored before you to open the door to God.

Moral Perspectives

SCCs among the first Jewish Christians also introduce a radically different moral code. Morality, hitherto, reflected behavior needed to preserve a tribal unity. The Ten Commandments, tribal laws codified hundreds of years before Moses by the Mesopotamian king, Hammurabi, served as a benchmark of moral behavior in pre-Christian times. Morality for the first SCCs, however, is summed up in one dictum: love God and neighbor as yourself. Morality seemed to be changed from the Old Testament commands of "you shall not" to "you shall," a shift from a prohibitive to a proactive orientation. Thus, behavior was elevated from tribal orientation reflected in the ten commandments to a new order reflected in the eight beatitudes.

Morality for the first SCCs was understood, not as a refraining from doing evil to neighbor, but of actively accepting neighbor with all the needs and limitations that neighbor may have. In so doing, SCC was prophetically revealing the suitor designs of God to accept the neighbor as beloved, regardless of the needs and limitations of the individuals involved. Thus SCCs were pursuing a morality far beyond that understood in ancient times and, in many cases, in modern times. Unity in your own SCC now becomes the benchmark for assessing morality. In the new order one becomes moral by doing something (reaching out to neighbor), not by refraining from violation of laws.

Theological Perspective

Theology, by definition, means "making sense out of our experience of God." In ancient times, as noted, believers tried to make sense of God in terms of making God identical to life itself. Four thousand years ago, Abraham rejected that image and laid the foundation for theologizing about God in terms of tribal chieftain who maintained unity through ten tribal laws. Finally, Christ introduced a new theology by defining God as a "coming together" of one's own person, whereby an experience of community (contrasted with membership in a tribe) is the result. A sense of community is directly related to responding to a divine election as beloved, initiated by a divine suitor.

This theology has been touched upon in previous chapters but bears repetition here because we are looking at it from another viewpoint, namely, in the context of the prophetic role of SCC. That prophetic role consists of pointing out what God is doing to an unbelieving world. SCC fulfills this prophetic mission, not by preaching but precisely by becoming SCC authentically reflecting the vision of unity revealed by Christ.

To put the theology as directly as possible: any influence toward unity that we experience is, in varying degrees, an experience of God because God alone is the author and source of communion. What determines the degree of God's presence is the degree to which "uniqueness of person, oneness in being and equality in majesty" is preserved. Your SCC, by reflecting communion at a personal level, is focused on unity at its deepest level. Thus, by achieving ever greater communion, becoming more like that found in the Trinity, your SCC is at the same time increasingly making sense of the experience of God. While the universal church is theologically understood as the enduring presence of God in human history, the SCC is the enduring presence of God in a particular time and place, with specific people and situations. The SCC makes God visible in direct proportion to the measure a given SCC radiates unity both within itself and to the neighbor touched by it. It is worthy of note that the potential of God's visibility is much greater at the personal level of SCC than at the administrative level of a world organization.

Sacramental Perspectives

Scripture reports that all were amazed at the first SCCs. Not only did members love one another but even before they came to know each other, they already loved one another. These early SCCs were acting as a sacrament in the community. In other words, these SCCs were making something sacred (sacra-) present (-ment) in a healing way. This is what "sacrament" means.

Your SCC is the greatest of all sacraments because it is a microcosm of the church and the continuation of the presence of Christ throughout history.

As we are wont to go to the sacraments for their beneficial and healing effects, so, too, anyone who draws near to your SCC ought to feel its healing effects. Your SCC is a sign to the world that God is present and healing.

It is easy to understand how the love radiated from your SCC is healing and life giving to those within range of its influence. But the sacramental effects are occurring within your SCC as well. Each member of your SCC also confers the life-giving sacrament of his or her own person on the others. This means that, as you yourself respond to your divine spouse, the love generated is transmitted to other members of your SCC in a unique way because your dialogue with your beloved is intimate and eminently personal. This sacramental love received by other members of your SCC has a great healing effect that goes beyond spiritual healing to envelop mental and physical levels as well. As members of your SCC are healed and made whole, they begin to extend to others the same healing action of God. In this way each of you and your SCC as a whole is fulfilling a sacramental mission by making visible God's determination to heal the human race.

Political Perspectives

It is safe to say that everyone throughout all history desires unity. The only problem is that each person wants it on his or her own terms. The history of the world may be viewed as competing drives toward unity. Each political system was created with a utopian notion of what sort of unity would be good for everyone. Those that do not fit in are often removed by execution, imprisonment, exile, excommunication, or eliminated in some other way to silence discord.

Every political system ever designed is doomed to implosion, undermined by a vision of unity more worthy of the human race. The most recent example is the implosion of the monolithic Communist empire that caved in almost overnight by its own dead weight. However, the sudden collapse must not make us forget the blood and suffering of millions over decades preparing the way for this historical event. The political order of the Communist world was based on the assumption that the basic identity of a human being is that of a "worker." The advent of individual "person" as a more worthy and fundamental reality upon which to build a world order penetrated the iron curtain and eventually brought about a collapse of the empire from within.

Your SCC is in this world and cannot be isolated from political pressures that are pushing for specific visions of what

constitutes the best order in human society. It has a role toward defining the best order for human beings. This is a prophetic endeavor because from the beginning God has been
working on a world order toward ultimate unity for humanity.
This unity alone is worthy of human beings.

We have witnessed during the past 70 years competing visions of unity that have slowly died. True unity based on love
must come from the bottom and cannot be imposed from the
top without violence erupting. When force is used, love cannot
abide. The SCC serves as a workshop through which individuals can come to a clear vision of a worthy world order. With
this clear vision, they can influence political institutions to
more adequately reflect human dignity and rights.

Teleological Perspective of Unity

Teleological means "making sense out of the end." In other
words, it tries to answer the question, what is the final destiny
of the human race? In a teleological sense, your SCC fulfills a
prophetic role of reaching beyond time to touch the espousal
God who gives meaning to the world. As every lover will at-
test, time melts away while in the embrace of the beloved. The
love affair initiated by God before time began, made visible in
Christ on Mt. Tabor, will someday envelop all who respond.
When this occurs, time will melt into eternity. On that day the
same communion that unites us to God will unite us to every
person who responded "yes" to the divine proposal.

Your SCC serves as a prophetic community by providing
now a small glimpse of the world that is coming, a world
pointed out by the ancient prophets, made manifest in Jesus
the beloved, and now quickened by the Spirit of Christ in your
SCC to hasten the final fulfillment.

It takes a lot of courage to let God be the source of unity.
We all are tempted to feel we know better, more practical
ways, especially when our patience is tried by the discord we
see everywhere. In essence, the teleological mission of your

SCC is allowing God to be God. In any love relationship, one spouse must never attempt to smother the other. If one decides how unity is to be achieved and impatiently resorts to force, such a person is assuming the identity and role of God.

Evolving Unity

We have taken you on a tour of unity from a variety of perspectives to make you aware that there is more to the experience of unity than a fuzzy good feeling. Your SCC has a prophetic role because Christ is a prime member who is present at your every gathering and is a prophet like no other.

It is important to realize that every union that is formed is destined to be broken up because all unions, however perfect they may seem, are only a shadow of the communion that is coming. We are strongly tempted to form unity too quickly, on a more or less shallow basis, because we are afraid of disunity. For this reason, members of SCC must acquire discipline as the basis of unity so that they can raise and discuss matters that are divisive, and rediscover unity at a still deeper level through the honest sharing of thoughts. If they rush toward unity prematurely they fall into the trap of patronizing. Discipline is required to achieve unity that will insure that God remains in the picture.

In Western culture, religion tends to degenerate into a complex code of moral laws that are used as standards against which to measure a person's degree of holiness or perversion. Christ's vision of religion transcends law. He was crucified because he was viewed as a threat to the holy laws of Judaism and therefore to the divine chieftain who gave the laws. Jesus points his disciples not to a codified set of laws, but toward a commitment to the "way," or simply to following him. Likewise, SCC is not a device to codify a set of laws to govern life but is an attempt to create a practical way to follow Christ in the world of today.

Christ is the first to practice the discipline required in coming together and by so doing invites every person throughout history to find his or her true self, as well as all who heed Christ's invitation. The process of coming together with our neighbor is going on now and will continue until the level of unity meets the standard set by Christ who laid down his life in our behalf.

Because the labor of coming together with neighbor demands a discipline beyond what law can require, bishops cannot legislate SCC as a requirement. Coming together can thrive only where persons acquire the discipline needed to overcome the obstacles that divide. Anyone who labors in SCC ministry easily recognizes the centrality of discipline and the need to exceed the demands of laws. The very fact that the love that binds your SCC together exceeds what any law can require or blood ties would expect is what makes SCC prophetically, to the new world that is coming, the kingdom of God.

To sum up the admonitions of this chapter, it is not enough to simply be a part of SCC; you must strive to understand its prophetic meaning. This takes a lot of work on your part but it is well worth the effort because a growing understanding provides clearer prophetic vision that leads to ever deeper levels of communion with God, other SCC members and your neighbor.

Conclusion

It should be clear that in accepting the presence of Jesus the beloved (Christ) as the leading member of your SCC, your SCC as a whole, and each individual member in it, are prophetic. Your participation in SCC becomes a lifestyle pointing to the new life God is anxious to pour into the world. The quickening of life draws all into a more perfect communion in which every wound will be healed and every tear wiped dry. The more conscious you are of your prophetic service to others by pointing out what God is doing, the more quickly resistance to the healing grace of God will evaporate.

You need not have the stature of such ancient prophets as Isaiah, Jeremiah, Ezekiel, or Daniel. Whatever you do, however small or insignificant, to manifest the abiding love of God seeking the beloved, is of the greatest importance. Where love is involved, the smallest things are paradoxically the greatest. In the next chapter we come to the threshold of a radically new perception of SCC based on Christ's role as the kingly servant. While the kingly servant perspective is different from the priest and prophet dimensions, it is, nevertheless, intimately associated with them.

This chapter may have introduced you to new territory. It is not easy to grasp the prophetic role that comes with being a follower of Christ. A series of questions and answers along with some discussion questions may help your SCC to sift through the implications of being a prophet in a darkened world.

QUESTIONS AND ANSWERS

Q. Politics is a game of power. How does our SCC fit into the drive for power?

A. With the same zeal that unbelievers seek to be number one, your SCC glories in its weakness. Faith ultimately requires the surrender of power over others. In so doing the creative influence of God is released as the divine spouse manifests in the beloved the glory of God hidden since time began. The transfiguration on Mt. Tabor is not an exercise of power over Jesus' disciples but reflects the influence of God being revealed in and through God's beloved spouse.

The dignity and worth of a person stems directly from the espousal relationship that God has initiated. This is true much the same way the dignity of Israel as a chosen people stems not from the tribe itself but from Yahweh who is perceived as chief. A person can rejoice in weakness because that very weakness constitutes an opening up to the fullness of life being poured forth from God.

The consequences of this way of thinking for your SCC are many. Perhaps the most important is that competition, which is the unquestioned foundation of the Western world, is categorically eliminated within and between small faith communities. One's worth need no longer be measured by possessions, social position, academic achievement, or the like. One need not feel discouraged if numbers are small or if progress is slow. In being the least of all, paradoxically, one gains a freedom and influence that is greater than all.

In short, your SCC is the presence of Christ in history. Although equal to God, he emptied himself and for this reason was exalted (Philippians 2:7). The small community of faith, for centuries rejected, may well reflect Christ who is also rejected by the builders. Like Christ, the humble SCC may well be destined to become the very corner stone of God's relationship with humankind in the modern world (Ephesians 2:20).

Q. How did we get away from the SCC structure of the church that prevailed for 300 years to the huge parish structures that we have today?

A. As mentioned in earlier chapters, the central dynamic of the apostolic church was dialogue (communion) that took place in homes of those attracted by the new found dignity expressed in the gospel. Dialogue and coming together are two sides of the same coin. This was quite obvious to the early Christians involved in SCCs.

However, when rich families who owned large houses were converted, the gatherings of believers became much larger causing dialogue to give way to discourse (testimonials by individuals) as a way of witnessing the faith (similar to modern day Pentecostal meetings). In the fourth century, the richest family of all (that of St. Helena and her son Constantine,

Emperor of Rome) was converted. Subsequently, pagan temples were confiscated and given to Christians to assemble in very large gatherings where discourse gave way to lectures on the "faith." In time, the successor to the fisherman from Galilee took on one of the titles of the Roman emperor: Sovereign Pontiff. As the church accumulated wealth, the role of the hierarchy was to oversee the distribution of funds, a practice that continues to the present day. Gradually, Mass and the sacraments were viewed as a system of grace to be administered by the hierarchy while the faithful became passive recipients.

Thus, in a brief moment of history, the SCC, which had survived for centuries and flourished in spite of vicious and unrelenting persecution, came to an abrupt end. To this day, many people think of church, not as a community first, but as a building with a hierarchy that manages real estate, personnel, and who say Mass and administer the sacraments.

To regain an effective voice in the rapidly changing world, the Catholic church is rediscovering its roots stemming from dialogue, the essential dynamic of the SCC. Throughout the world, small communities are emerging as a basic structure of the Catholic church, because it is only at this level that dialogue is possible. Gatherings are based on the level of dialogue sought or attained, not on artificially imposed requirements. As SCC grows in size, it often divides into two or more communities out of the need to preserve communion (i.e., dialogue).

Q. You refer to SCC as church. Can you give more background on the use of the term "church"?

A. As early as 400 B.C. Greeks invented a new concept of government based on the assumption that all adult males should have an equal voice in conducting the affairs of the city. The Greeks believed that in so doing each male would have a vested interest in fighting to defend the city. To achieve this goal, they instituted a "church" (coined by the Greeks to signify a "calling together"). While at church the males of the city had opportunity to discuss and vote on issues that affected their lives and at the same time learned of any dangers threatening their city.

About 500 years after the ancient Greeks had instituted the first church, the early Jewish Christians adopted the Greek concept of church as ideally suited to highlight their belief that each disciple is equally responsible as collaborators with Christ to come together in a continuing effort to make all things whole. Christians expanded the Greek concept of city to encompass the whole world. Thus to the first Christians, a "church" meant a "world," or "catholic," church.

In so doing, the Jewish Christians rejected the familiar nomenclature "synagogue" (Hebrew word meaning assembly). These first Christians chose the name of church, not only to distinguish themselves from Jewish assemblies (synagogues), but also to focus on coming together (beyond the tribal sense characteristic of Judaism), as a universal calling in which there was to be no distinction between male or female, slave or free, Jew or Gentile (Galatians 3:28). This unprecedented "calling together" for dialogue (communio in Latin) was soon to constitute the very essence of Christian belief and practice. Consequently, shortly after apostolic times, many began to join the word "catholic" (Greek word meaning universal) to the word "church," when referring to Christian gatherings. The words Catholic church became short for "coming together of everyone" or "coming together regardless of who you are."

By adopting the Greek concept of church, the first Christians implied that church is more than an assembly or a hierarchial organization (an image exaggerated later in the minds of some even to the point of replacing the original notion of church with the image of a Christian army). Nor do the words group, meeting or family adequately convey the meaning of church because they do not define the inner meaning of the gathering. To repeat for emphasis what was said in an earlier chapter, for a disciple of Christ, "church" signifies a coming together occurring at least on three levels: 1) the physical act of coming together to a designated point; 2) the coming together of a number of persons whose lives flow together like rivulets into one stream; and 3) the interior coming together of the persona of each believer to new dimensions of life and peace on a journey to meet face to face the God of the risen Christ.

Q. Do I understand this chapter right: If I go to work Monday morning and make a special effort to wish a cheerful good morning to my co-workers, I thereby exercise a prophetic role?

A. Yes, and you would probably do it even more if you backed your words up with a box of donuts to share with co-workers as a surprise. Let us define again that a prophet is one who points by word or action to what God is doing here and now in God's eternal design to make all things one, with God being the cause and source of that unity. Thus, just as a cup of cold water offered to the thirsty will not go unnoticed, your cheerful "good morning" contributes in a small but important way to drawing people together.

Your SCC can be far more effective if you are conscious of this prophetic dimension of your words and actions. Be ever mindful, however, that your prophetic initiative is not the cause of solidarity among members of your SCC or among co-workers, but rather the opening of the door at a particular time and place that enables God to draw all of us together.

Q. Doesn't it trivialize the notion of being a prophet to view it in terms of everyday life, to say that we can be prophets in our daily words and actions?

A. Nothing could be more commonplace than for a middle-aged woman, tired from a hard day at work, to remain seated on a bus. Yet that one action of Rosa Parks opened the door to one of the greatest civil rights movements in history. From the beginning it has been the design of God to bring all people together. The "trivial" action of this humble woman opened the door to God's greater involvement in human history.

Rosa Parks at the time may not have been aware of the prophetic nature of her act. She may have been just too tired or just fed up with the idea that a black woman must yield her seat to a white man. God can bring about unity even if we are unconscious of God's plan. God's work would be greatly accelerated, however, if we became more aware of our prophetic role, one that is clearly revealed in Christ. Since SCC, by definition, is prophetic, your SCC will survive and prosper only to the degree that it grows to an awareness of its prophetic mission of demonstrating here and now the design of unity that God has in store for all of humanity.

Q. Christ actually caused disunity. He even said that he came to set one member of a family at odds with another, father against son, daughter against mother. How do you explain this in keeping with the concept of prophecy as pointing toward unity?

A. A prophetic word or action, to be prophetic, leads to greater unity because it is a sign of God's presence and life. Christ came that we may have life and have it to the full. However, God as life and a person's notion of life are not identical. Herein lies the problem.

Christ himself resisted the conventional idea that unity comes from political institutions, no matter how strongly supported with the sword or loftily clothed in religious ideas or ideals. Rather, it is God who is the architect of unity and the design of God goes beyond the tribe of the Jews to include the whole of humanity. Enraged at such a heretical notion, Jesus' own people rose up to expel him. In his crucifixion, Jesus succeeds in pointing to love (there is no greater love than to lay down one's life for another) as the only worthy image of God from which comes both unity and life. Abraham, Moses, Jesus, and the great prophets of history did not wish to cause disunity but to enhance the life of the world.

Our conventional notions of unity do not always encompass true unity. When conventional notions are challenged, many get very upset. Thirty years ago when SCCs began in parishes, many viewed them as disruptive, if not outright heretical. Now that SCC is becoming more and more the conventional way for parishes to go, the new danger is closing our eyes to the next step for introducing God to our modern world. A SCC is but another step toward unity, not the final one.

Q. Are you suggesting that we try to be unconventional in order to fulfill our prophetic calling?

A. Not at all. Being unconventional is not the cause of unity but is sometimes the unavoidable consequence of it. When you love your enemy or do good to those who hate you, you are breaking with convention. Your behavior may cause further aggravation, but that is not your intention. Christ's love infuriated his enemies but Christ continued to do good because he knew it to be the pathway to the living God.

Every day we are faced with being unconventional. Recall our words in chapter one about the uniqueness of every person. Simply by accepting each person as a unique manifestation of God's espousal love, you are being unconventional. At the same time you are opening the door for others to increase life by accepting themselves as worthy of God's love. Thus, your SCC need not be out looking for unconventional things to do.

To continue this thought, each person we meet leads us to a unique experience of our own persona in a way no other person can. When you open yourself to another person, it is not a situation of one plus one equals two, but one plus one equals a new universe. You are like a musical instrument on which every person who comes into your life plays a unique and exquisite melody that only that person can play. There is nothing conventional about your deepest identity.

To carry this thought just one step further, your SCC is like no other gathering in all history because it is made up of unique persons. Thus, it should be apparent that we don't have to try to be or do something unconventional to be prophetic. As we continue to open up to the living God all human conventions will melt away.

Q. I learned in my catechism that Jesus is priest, prophet, and king. Isn't it enough simply to acknowledge that truth?

A. Truth is useless without understanding. Many find comfort in knowing that they have the truth, or belong to the true religion or to an infallible church. Truths, however, are like treasures that are buried and must be sought, dug up, and appreciated. Your SCC provides you with that opportunity.

There have been many heated discussions of how God fits into our lives. These debates about God and God's designs for the world can be eased by reflecting on a simple rule of thumb: give God credit for being as smart as you are. After all, God created intelligence so God must have at least as much of it as we do.

Each of us have a conscious (or at least an unconscious) image of God that governs our life. If technology could take these deep seated images and project them on a screen, we might be shocked at our own notion of God—and not a little embarrassed. Undoubtedly you can think of someone you know who behaves as if God were a ruthless taskmaster ready to punish the smallest failing. Such a person would not do that to their own children. Thus, the personal image of this person is better than the image he or she has of God.

Your SCC need not be afraid to delve more deeply into the truths each member holds so dearly, if you just stop from time to time to apply the above simple rule of thumb. You will discover how intelligent God really is. It is too bad that many of our modern television evangelists don't take time to apply this simple rule of thumb to what they are saying about God.

Q. How can I avoid becoming a false prophet by saying or doing something that appears to be leading to unity and life, but in reality is leading to disunity and destruction?

A. The answer is simple and close at hand. Stay in dialogue with your SCC. Christ is not a passive but a very active member of your SCC. He is very much involved in the dialogue and will in due time lead you to an understanding of all that he has received from God.

While this answer is simple enough, remember that the achievement of dialogue is far from simple. Members are in constant danger of falling into a monologue as individuals, thus creating a paralysis that can spread through the whole community. This leads your SCC toward a phenomenon called "groupthink," in which monologue is generalized within the whole group. As individuals, we tend to shut out things that are disturbing and latch onto things that confirm our viewpoint. When this is extended to a group as a whole, the group thinks as an individual. What appears to be a dialogue because of the number of persons involved is, in reality, a monologue, because all contrary evidence is consciously or unconsciously excluded.

The chances are that a group that is characterized by monologue will not stand the test of time. The point is, your SCC is an excellent workshop for dialogue. Its purpose is not to formulate an ideology. Through dialogue you will discover many delightful things about yourself, and at times also painful things. Your full and honest participation in your SCC is the best guarantee that your vision of unity will be from God and not an empty illusion.

Q. When do we know that our SCC has arrived, so to speak?

A. In the Western world we tend to view life as a series of goals to be reached, when all will then be perfect. The goals in our life may be graduating from college, landing a good job, getting a promotion, paying off the mortgage, or the arrival of a grandchild. When we get there we discover that all is not as perfect as we anticipated. So we search for another goal. We seem incapable of living in the present.

Do not make the same mistake with your SCC. When your parish has been subdivided into SCCs, or when you finally grasp the theology of SCC, or when SCC has become a diocesan priority, things will still not be perfect. Look at each gathering of your SCC as unique, as if it were the very first meeting, no matter how many years it has been in existence. Much has happened since you last gathered. Each meeting then is in a real sense like a first meeting, because each member has been changed by intervening events. Each gathering is a moment of grace for those present and a loss to those who are not. Thus, in SCC you are forever arriving but at the same time forever departing for a new world of intimacy with God and all who seek this divine suitor.

Q. I had 12 years of Catholic education. Why wasn't I taught about SCC as a child?

A. Throughout history the church has emphasized those elements of the gospel that are most helpful for meeting the needs of a given generation or era. Today the dignity of the individual and enduring family relationships are being threatened by a modern technological revolution. SCC, with its theology of person and relationship, provides the emphasis on the truths we need today to survive the deluge of impersonalization.

You were not taught about SCC as a child because the need for the theology that surrounds it was not yet apparent. Furthermore, understanding SCC is beyond the comprehension of a child because dialogue that is central to SCC requires the maturity of an adult.

QUESTIONS FOR REVIEW AND DISCUSSION

1. What does an "increase in life" mean? Give examples. What effect does this increase have on unity? Can it be the cause of disunity?

2. What is meant by the teleological dimension of SCC? Can you realistically imagine a bond greater than that of blood?

3. SCC introduces a new morality. What does this mean in theory and in practice?

4. Your SCC is a sacrament, the greatest of all sacraments, because from it comes all other sacraments. What does this mean?

5. Trace the historical development of SCC. What were the major breakthroughs in our imaging of God?

6. What do we mean when we say God alone is the source and cause of unity for humankind? What are the implications? Be specific.

7. What does being a prophet today mean? How can you be prophetic? How does the prophetic role differ from the priestly role?

8. In Old Testament times sin was viewed as a violation of a law. What new understanding of sin does the prophetic mission of Christ offer?

9. Why are prophecy and unity two sides of the same coin?

10. Can unity be achieved on a global scale? Why or why not?

Chapter 6

My Soul
Magnifies the Lord

The title "kingly servant" appears to be an oxymoron because king and servant are on opposite ends of the social spectrum. Being a king means that others are expected to cater to one's every whim in order to receive a special favor. Suggestion that being a king is equivalent to being a servant is a contradiction in terms. However, this enigmatic designation of kingly servant is applied to Christ, and therefore to your SCC because it is an extension of Christ in history. Although "kingly servant" is a difficult concept, the struggle to understand it is well worth your effort.

Part of the confusion can be resolved by recalling that being a king in ancient times was tantamount to being the author or originator of life for all who lived in the king's realm. When the king died, the entire world, which was considered to be coextensive with the particular king's realm, came to an end, including even the reckoning of time. When a new king emerged, year one began again and a new world came into being that again lasted only until the death of the king. A king not only totally dominated but was thought to be the very source of the life and thought of his realm. Ancient records remain of kings and kingdoms, but because they do not make reference to events outside a particular kingdom, it is difficult or impossible to date those events according to our calendar, which is based on the birth of Christ. Our calendar begins with Christ because his followers perceived him to be a new king and therefore the originator of a new order (kingdom). Unlike any other king in history, however, when the title of king is applied to Christ, it is hyphenated with "servant."

Jesus as Kingly Servant

The first Christians saw Christ as king, that is, the originator of life. At the same time, they saw him as a king who willingly became the lowliest servant to the very least in an effort to lead them to life. In effect, although Christ remains our king, he makes even the lowliest among us his king, begging each to accept the gift of life as a special favor to him. This marks the beginning of a new order, where kingship is conferred upon all of us through the servant role that Christ the king assumes. Jesus turns our world, which is based on an order achieved through power and privilege, upside down. Henceforth the greatest in this new world order is the person who is the servant of all.

SCC as Kingly Servant

Now that we have some notion of Christ as kingly servant, how do you recognize the kingly servant dimension of your SCC? This is a difficult connection to make, perhaps even more difficult than seeing your SCC in its priestly and prophetic role, as discussed in previous chapters. However, understanding the kingly servant facet of your SCC will provide you with a three-dimensional view, namely, a view of your SCC as priest, prophet, and kingly servant. This three-dimensional perspective is absolutely necessary if you are to perceive your SCC as the continuation of the real presence of Christ in the modern world.

Understanding your kingly servant role will take a considerable amount of careful reflection on your part, as well as patience and persistence. To begin, you must step back from your SCC and discover that the kingly servant characteristic is in itself a three-dimensional reality. After you are comfortable in doing this, you can proceed to take a closer look at how the kingly servant phenomenon, or event, within your SCC is applied in practice.

In the kingly servant phenomenon (event) there are three simultaneous dynamics: 1) giving, 2) surge of life, 3) receiving. Your SCC comes together precisely for the purpose of making these three elements operative. In so doing it makes Christ the kingly servant present in time and place, and allows his healing mission to continue.

Let us get our bearings on the meaning of the kingly servant phenomenon within your SCC today by taking a closer look at the early SCCs. As the first SCCs began to gather in apostolic times, the extension of the healing power of Christ was a dominant concern, not only because of the many physical and social ills of that day, but also because healing attracts people to Christ. How important this preoccupation with healing was becomes readily apparent when you recall that accounts of what Jesus said and did, as recorded in the gospels, were in reality a reflection of the early SCCs trying to sort out who Jesus was, as well as their own identity as the continuation of the healing Christ.

The idea of actually writing down favorite memories of the healing events in the public ministry of Christ came many years later after the death of Jesus. This was something of an afterthought, a way for early SCCs to preserve their collective memories and experiences of Jesus for future generations. The first SCCs were, however, much more concerned about continuing the word of the healing Christ than they were with writing about Christ. In other words, these first SCCs saw themselves as the continuation of the healing Christ who was perceived as very much alive and among them.

There is some truth in saying that the gospels are concerned primarily with defining what the kingly servant role of Christ is and, by extension, what the kingly servant role of your SCC is. The authenticity of Christ, and by extension, of your SCC, comes precisely from the king-servant phenomenon. Through the kingly servant role, your SCC becomes visible for all the world to see and reckon with. When your SCC offers healing, people will sit up and take notice. It should be obvious how important it is to understand the kingly servant power of your SCC. Perhaps the best way to gain an understanding is to look at a few illustrations of how the kingly servant phenomenon is recorded in Scripture.

Annunciation and Visitation

Recall for a moment the annunciation and visitation events as reported in Luke's gospel. At the annunciation, Mary is informed that she is to be the mother of Jesus. The "visitation" refers to Mary's visit to her cousin Elizabeth who is pregnant with John the Baptist. Mary becomes aware of the pregnancy of Elizabeth at the time of the annunciation and immediately goes to care for Elizabeth's needs because Elizabeth is advanced in years. When Mary (the giver) arrives, the baby in Elizabeth's womb leaps for joy (surge of life, i.e., the presence of God) and Elizabeth (the receiver) cries out wondering why the mother of her Lord has come to serve her? All three elements of the kingly servant phenomenon (giver, surge of life and receiver) are present in this account. The reaction to its presence is the response given by Mary in her Magnificat, the most beautiful verbalization ever of what the experience is like when God, the kingly servant par excellence, is suddenly present in human events.

Note in this event that Mary the giver is both king ("king" meaning "originator" of life) and servant; the involvement of God, in the form of the infant leaping in Elizabeth's womb, has both a king and servant dimension. Elizabeth is approached as "king" but insists on her servant relationship to Mary in these words: "Who am I that the mother of my lord comes to wait on me." For the kingly servant event to take place, all three (giver, God, and receiver) must be present simultaneously as king and servant.

SCC creates an environment where this is possible. Whenever the kingly servant phenomenon is present, the excitement reflected in the Magnificat is also present. In one way or another, both the giver and receiver have the urge to cry out with Mary, "My soul magnifies the lord, and my spirit rejoices in God my savior." In each such event the espousal relationship of God becomes a little clearer. The spirit of the Magnificat should, in time, become the predominant and enduring experience of SCC because it dwells at the very center of God's healing action in the world.

Wedding Feast at Cana

Another example may help to clarify the pattern of three (giver, God, and receiver) being simultaneously present to bring about the phenomenon of healing. The pattern is exemplified at the beginning of Jesus' public ministry at a wedding feast. At the height of the celebration the wine runs out, causing great embarrassment to the host. Mary (giver) responds to the situation by instructing a waiter to do whatever Jesus suggests. Jesus asks the waiter to fill large stone jars with water and then to draw some out and take it to the head steward (receiver).

Because of the presence of Christ (God's surge of life), the water had become the finest wine. The head steward, after tasting the water made into wine, breaks out in praise (the Magnificat effect), and immediately runs to the host protesting that this good wine should have been served first and poor wine later when palates had become dulled.

The gospel writers framed the beginning of Christ's public ministry at a wedding feast undoubtedly to highlight that a successful marriage has to embody a king-servant relationship if life is to flow between the couple and from them to new offspring. The first SCCs preserved this memory of Christ at the marriage feast of Cana because it reflects so well the changing of the water of human love into a new wine of intoxicating love experienced in the Christian community. This is made possible because of the presence of Christ (surge of life) who participates in every gathering.

It should be noted that the changing of water into wine is not used by Jesus to prove his divine mission. No miracle performed by him was ever used by him to prove anything. Jesus resisted a temptation from Satan to throw himself from the pinnacle of the temple to prove to everyone that he was from God. All the miracles Jesus performed were focused on healing others and it was precisely in this healing that he found the means to reveal his true identity as the beloved of God and to vindicate his mission.

In recording the healing effects of Christ, the first SCCs were in effect talking about the healing effects that emanated from the SCC to the community. The first SCCs saw their identity as the continuation of the miracle of healing initiated by Christ. For this to occur, however, all three elements of the kingly servant phenomenon reflected in the two examples just given had to be present.

Multiplication of the Loaves and Fishes

One more example from the gospels may help you grasp the miraculous potential of your SCC. Crowds of people followed Jesus for days, hanging on his every word, not even taking time to eat. Jesus pointed out to his disciples that the people were hungry, but his disciples protested they had nothing to give this crowd numbering in the thousands. However, a young man was there with a few loaves of bread and some fish.

Once again the classic kingly servant phenomenon is present: A young man with a small amount of bread and fish (giver), a hungry crowd (receiver), and twelve baskets of bread and fish left over after all had eaten (surge of life which reflects the presence of God in the person of Christ). The Magnificat effect is reflected in the uncontrollable amazement of the crowd and the need for Jesus to flee, lest the crowds take him by force to make him king.

Other examples from the gospels can be cited and you may wish to review them with the above paradigm in mind. What is important is that you recognize the kingly servant potential of your SCC. The presence of Christ in your SCC brings all the healing power reflected in the Scriptures into the present. You hold in your hands as SCC the key to unlocking the healing power of a loving God.

Love as the Inner Dynamic

Simply giving something to another in need is not a kingly servant act. Saint Paul, in one of his most eloquent moments, tries to show the necessary connection between giving something and the underlying love (presence of Christ) that draws SCC together. He writes, "If I distribute all my goods to feed the poor, and if I deliver my body to be burned, yet do not have love it profits me nothing. Love is patient, is kind; love does not envy, is not pretentious, is not puffed-up, is not ambitious, is not self-seeking, is not provoked; thinks no evil, does not rejoice over wickedness, but rejoices with the truth; bears all things, believes all things, hopes all things, endures all things" (1 Corinthians 13:3-7).

Paul, as well as John the evangelist, frequently equates love with the presence of God, but this version of love far surpasses that of a Hollywood variety. Moreover, the servant role that stems from love includes less visible healing, such as rendering to others a service of patience, kindness, forbearance, inspiration of hope, and a willingness to rejoice with the truth.

These and many other types of service are an important part of the kingly servant role of an SCC. When love (God) is present in a kingly servant event, the healing power of God is released through the giver to the receiver of the service. The presence of God through love insures the dignity of the recipient. The left hand of the giver must not know what the right hand is doing. In a kingly servant event all three, giver, God, and receiver are both king and servant. In SCC it is a win-win situation for all.

Sign of True Church

There are thousands of SCCs in the world today. How are we to know that any particular one is authentically the presence of Christ and not just some sort of therapy group or a group of compatible people who enjoy talking about God or life in general together? There were thousands of small groups in apostolic times that were devoted to a variety of cults. How did the first Christians solve the problem of distinguishing which groups were indeed led by the Spirit of Christ?

The one distinguishing sign that set SCC apart from counterfeits was the kingly servant characteristic. A counterfeit group was incapable of a kingly servant event because bad trees cannot produce good fruit. The first Christians fully realized how the kingly servant characteristic set SCC apart from every other group. This awareness characteristic of true SCC was described by Jesus himself. The disciples of John the Baptist came to him to ask if he was indeed the messiah who was to come or if they should be looking for another? Jesus replied: "Go back and report to John what you have heard and seen:

the blind see, the lame walk, the lepers are cleansed, the deaf hear, the dead rise, and the poor have the gospel preached to them" (Matthew 11:4-5).

In the minds of the first Christians, healing is the acid test of authenticity. If Jesus did not bring about healing in society, he would have been dismissed as just another of the hundreds of learned rabbis who had a theory about God and what God expected. This same acid test must be used with your SCCs which reveal the risen Christ living today. The first SCCs never thought of Jesus as someone who had died, but as one alive then and there through the SCC. In like manner we must believe that Jesus is present here and now through our SCCs. If this is not so, Christ is truly dead and his enemies have indeed triumphed over him.

What the gospels are saying of Jesus they are saying of our SCCs which by definition make present the risen Christ in a particular time and place. It might also be added that what the enemies of Jesus did to him they will do to him again as he lives in SCC. However, through our SCCs, the healing power of Jesus will continue and will be evidence that an espousal, healing God continues to sweep us off our feet toward a destiny that surpasses our wildest imagination. We, in turn, will be unable to resist responding in the spirit of the Magnificat.

The endless giving that is an essential part of the kingly servant role should not be cause for fear but should come as great consolation as we struggle to develop SCCs. We do not have to "prove" anything to anyone about our SCCs. The healing power that flows from them will be ample proof that Christ is in our midst. But, while we are healing others, we ourselves will experience healing effects because a kingly servant event opens the door to the creative action of God who seeks to make all things whole. God cannot do so without our cooperation.

Does this mean that we must give all our possessions to feed the poor in order to insure that the presence of Christ will be manifested in our SCCs? No, although members of the first SCCs in apostolic times did exactly that, though it led to more problems than it solved. When SCCs become preoccupied with raising and giving away money, attention becomes more focused on care and administration of material goods then on the presence of Christ. The kingly servant characteristic of SCC is much more complex than just making contributions. As indicated above, Paul saw healing as more than simply filling hungry stomachs. Besides hunger there are much deeper needs like blindness, deafness, deadness, and despair. Responding to these deeper needs will also lead to healing of the more superficial needs.

Need for Awareness

If you are going to be adept in detecting a kingly servant event, you must first of all become a keen observer. Look for the kingly servant phenomenon first within your SCC. Healing will occur before your eyes. This healing may be manifested in the form of a growing peace or joy radiated by a member who formerly was burdened with confusion, hopelessness, or depression. The healing may create a generous giving spirit in one who formerly clung to possessions. It may be manifested simply in a greater air of freedom that a member may begin to display. A great desire to come together as SCC in itself is indication that a deep healing is going on that no one is quite able to put into words.

Healing in SCC operates on many levels. Thus, if a member goes out of his or her way to find a job for a down and out person, healing is taking place. However, it would be a much greater healing if your SCC also restored enough hope in the unemployed person to enable him or her to locate a job on his or her own. Or, if a member is nursing a grudge, or anger, prejudice, or greed, healing is needed on a deeper level because this person has an unseen spiritual cancer. A person will never know a forgiving God unless that individual experiences what it means to forgive another. Your SCC creates an atmosphere for this to happen.

Not only should you be observant of small signs of healing in your SCC, but you should also share what you have seen happening in yourself or others. In so doing, other members will become more aware of the kingly servant phenomenon and be witnesses to the enduring evidence that Christ the healer still lives.

There may also be dramatic healing episodes, but don't look for them. Our notion of big may not be the same as God's notion. A change of heart that opens one to life is the greatest miracle of all. Thus, it is unlikely that your SCC will lay hands on a corpse, dead for three days, and bring it back to life as Jesus brought Lazarus back from the dead. Learn, rather, to recognize signs that lead to death. A person may be secretly considering suicide because life is too burdensome or meaningless. Your SCC may in fact raise such a person from the dead by leading him or her to the excitement of discovering an espousal God.

Blindness of the soul is worse than blindness of the eyes. Deafness of the spirit is worse than deafness in the ears. People with such afflictions are all candidates for healing. Your SCC is the kingly servant empowered by Christ to heal. Remember, we are all poor in the measure that we do not hear the good news (gospel) of our election by an espousal God. It is like carrying a winning Lotto ticket worth millions in your pocket and never discovering your good fortune. The greatest healing of all is when our SCCs radiate both within and without that life is an exciting, loving dialogue between each person and a wonderful and tender God. As SCCs, there is no limit to the power of our healing because our SCCs bring the presence of God effectively into human history in a specific time, place, and situation.

Befriending the Stranger
The central mission of your SCC is that of befriending the

stranger. Being strangers is the first direct effect of sin, as reflected in the ancient story of Cain turning away from his
brother Abel. We will be less and less strangers to one another
as the God who espouses each of us is revealed. Reducing the
gap that separates us one from another is the most important
healing that must take place.

The first outward evidence that you have discovered the
love initiative of God on your behalf is your open response to
a stranger or "neighbor" (as the gospels generally refer to the
people we meet every day and who may be unknown or
known only superficially to us). Fear of the unknown paralyz-
es us. People are free to extend a new loving openness to their
neighbors only when they have become more alive to their unknown but unique worth as the beloved of God.

The interplay of the discovery of self-worth, and consequently that of one's neighbor, is the basis for participation in
larger gatherings of believers at the regional (parish), national,
or international levels. Befriending the stranger also has the
beneficial (sacramental) effect of discovering new dimensions
of our own persona. The befriending in turn may spark a discovery in the stranger of the divine courtship in his or her behalf that began before the mountains were set in their place or
rivers were confined to their banks (Proverbs 8:22).

The opposite of befriending is ostracising ("excommunica-
ion," from the Latin). This practice, invented by the ancient
Greeks, involved calling the community together to vote on
banishing a member because of an offence. It was inconceivable among the ancient Greeks, however, that a person would
be banished (made a stranger) for more than two or three
months, even for very serious offenses.

Later Christian adaptation, however, exaggerated the original Greek concept. This resulted in excommunication that often endured for centuries (e.g., Martin Luther) and often was
based, not on the vote of the community, but on the decision of
a very few. For the SCC, which draws its very life from be-

friending the alienated, ostracism makes no sense. Besides, Christians, by definition, view the entire world as a community. The ancient Greeks sent the undesirable outside the city walls. Christians cannot do this.

If a person withdraws from participation in the life of SCC, it must be the result of the person's own decision. Nor is there call for judgment toward such a person since God alone sees the heart of each person. Failure to offer friendship on a continuing basis, however, would be a fatal blow to the inner life of SCC, of which Christ himself is a member.

Conclusion

In the fast pace of life, people have been increasingly confronted with the disturbing questions, Who am I? What is the image I have of myself? Many successfully dodge the question until a catastrophe strikes their lives, such as being replaced at their job by a machine that is more accurate and efficient than they are. A displaced, unemployed worker is often forced to ask for the first time, Who am I? Am I of less value than the machine that can perform so much better?

Your SCC must constantly struggle with this same question of identity: Who am I? Christ is not dead but is risen and is playing a very active part in your SCC. As your SCC puts on Christ as priest, prophet, and kingly servant, Christ will become increasingly visible to you and to the world, enabling him to continue his work of loving, healing, and wiping away every tear.

If you find it difficult to sort out your identity as SCC, take heart; this is a gradual process. If you were to instantly see yourself as God sees you, you would be so overwhelmed by such love that you would be immobilized. Furthermore, the transformation that would occur in you would be so disconcerting to your family and friends who often feel that they are in competition with you.

Competition is often used as a short-cut to an identity but

it is one built on shifting sand. Jesus saw clearly who he was, and as a consequence saw no need to lord it over others. His example embarrassed those among his followers who competed for recognition. The leaders of the people put him to death for fear his status as the beloved of God would upset the tribal unity they sought. Therefore, be patient, remembering that every new insight into your identity will have consequences. God is well aware of our frailty and will not allow more awareness than we can bear.

It is time now to pause for more in-depth understanding of the kingly servant role of your SCC. The following questions and answers will help stimulate discussion in your SCC on this vital issue. A list of group discussion questions aimed at reviewing the kingly servant dimension of your SCC, concludes this chapter.

QUESTIONS AND ANSWERS

Q. How did we as church get so far away from the kingly servant role?

A. Healing as a key characteristic of the church has always been implicit in her teaching and explicit in the theology of the sacrament of the sick. Christians have long believed that the anointing of the body of a sick person heals the soul, and at times the body as well.

However, the time is ripe to bring out in the open again the church's implicit teaching about healing. People today are becoming increasingly isolated from one another, and poverty, drugs, and violence are rampant. The time is right for reversing this alienation from one another and consequently from God, by refocusing on the kingly servant "healing" characteristic of the church in SCC.

Q. Does our SCC have power to perform miracles just like Christ did?

A. No, it has power to perform even greater miracles. Jesus himself said, "Those who believe in me, the works that I do so also will they and greater than these shall they do" (John 14:12). "Miracle" means a special intervention of God in a particular situation. The constant lesson of history is that God gladly intervenes but does not use force. The problem is that we do not know how to create a situation that is inviting to God's action.

If we are distressed by our violent and chaotic world, it is symptomatic of the failure of SCCs to open the door to God to enter human affairs. A spouse cannot force him or herself on the beloved. Therefore, God is a helpless outsider until someone opens a door from within. In your SCC you may have been able to identify occasions when there has been a "special intervention" of God. As your SCC continues to develop, you will become even more aware of a continuous interplay between God and your SCC.

Q. I can't believe that SCC can perform miracles of physical healing. Can you cite an instance?

A. An instance that readily comes to mind occurred when a distraught mother brought her infant with severe brain damage to her neighborhood SCC. The doctor gave the mother little or no hope that the infant would ever be able to function independently. The SCC responded to the need by arranging a regimen of stimulation to develop the undamaged portion of the child's brain. Members of the SCC arranged their schedules so each could work with the child during its early years to provide the needed stimulation. To the amazement of the doctor, the child responded and was able to achieve a remarkable measure of independence and normalcy.

An event need not be dramatic to be termed a miracle. God does not perform miracles like a magician in a sideshow at a circus. Miracles require a three dimensional partnership in which giver, God, and receiver are equally king and servant.

Q. If belonging to an SCC has such great potential, why doesn't the church make it a requirement?

A. Force cannot be the basis of SCC. That would be like a shotgun marriage. Those entering into SCC are responding to an espousal image of God that necessarily leads to spiritual relationships with other members. Personal freedom is paramount. Each must respond when and to the degree that he or she is ready. Pushing or rushing everyone into SCC only serves to muddy the waters. God can operate by invitation only; the same goes with all of us in our relationship to one another.

Q. If our SCC becomes a leading influence in our neighborhood, parish, or community, won't others take advantage of our willingness to give, thus leading to the burnout of our SCC?

A. This can happen. Jesus cautions us to be simple as doves but wise as serpents (Matthew 10:16). The kingly servant phenomenon requires the willing involvement of giver and receiver as a precondition for the involvement of God in an event. Wise as serpents means the ability to spot the patronizer and con artist no matter what guise or ruse may be used. An ability to share in SCC that preserves dignity and reciprocity is a skill that requires endless discipline and patience.

Remember, too, that conning can go on inside as well as outside your SCC, and it can be for money or non-material things such as recognition, power, prestige, or advantage over others, all of which lead to disruption of dialogue. Surviving as SCC in itself requires a tremendous level of self-giving. Learn to be wise as serpents in giving, but simple as doves when it comes to inviting deeper involvement.

Q. I have never thought of patronizing as a form of conning. When you caution SCC to beware of patronizing, what do you mean?

A. An espousal perception of God is the highest form of imaging the divine-human relationship ever attained in the history of the world. Your SCC has as its sole purpose to create an environment in which an individual can nurture an awareness of being called to espousal communion with God as the beloved of God. Patronizing means using your SCC for any other purpose.

The divine-human dialogue that occurs in your SCC is the source of life, not only for your SCC, but for all organizations, religious or secular, that relate to it. Your SCC gives meaning to the world because it is the point of contact between a person, God, and neighbor. For the believer, this encounter in your SCC is the holy of holies as much as the sanctuary in the temple was the holy of holies to the ancient Israelites, because therein dwelt God the divine chieftain of their tribe. When Jesus died, the curtain of that sanctuary was torn from top to bottom, thus indicating that the presence of God is to be sought elsewhere. Your SCC is the new dwelling place of God and, accordingly, is deserving of the greatest reverence. All the world is called to revere the divine-human dialogue that is unfolding and to support the transformation (transfiguration) that is occurring in your SCC.

Those persons who cling to a tribal notion of God, that is, the notion that God is a divine chieftain who has handed down laws for tribal members to follow, or those who assume God is identical to life itself (thought by some to be the basis of Hinduism) are more likely to be patronizing toward SCC based on an espousal image of God. In essence, patronizing is a display of ignorance regarding the massive investment involved in creating SCC. As Christ so aptly pointed out, "Many are called but few are chosen" (Matthew 20:16). Many follow Christ like tribal members following a leader because that requires only the fulfillment of a code of conduct. Few are willing to pursue the struggle of coming to grips with the call to be the chosen beloved of God.

Q. I have noticed that some parishioners look at our SCC with suspicion. Is the alienation that we feel a part of that "giving" you speak of in our kingly servant role?

A. Your understanding is correct. A feeling of alienation for SCC is "normal." Abraham was alienated because he reacted to the prevailing beliefs of his time; the Israelites were alienated because they sought freedom from the slavery imposed upon them; Christ was alienated because of his espousal image of God in a tribal culture. A feeling of alienation is merely a negative way of looking at your experience of uniqueness as an individual or as SCC.

If indeed a person is defined as a unique entity then one can expect hostility from those who feel we all ought to be the same in every way. We are not all the same. Indeed, none of us are alike. If we were, there would be no need for God in the Christian viewpoint because, as indicated in the previous chapter, God is defined as the center of gravity drawing us into unity. God alone is author of unity. Remember that a patient acceptance of alienation serves as an occasion for God to reveal the unique espousal relationship to which you have been called. Don't over-react to the misunderstanding of others. Patient love will eventually touch even the hardest of hearts, but a word spoken in anger will only close minds tighter.

Q. Giving seems to take many forms. The more we gather as SCC the more we see what is lacking in the church as a whole. Is patience with church leaders an aspect of the "giving" you speak of?

A. If you understand your SCC in its priestly, prophetic, and kingly servant identity as presented in the last three chapters, you can easily become critical of "church" as a local, regional, national, and world organization. When you understand the espousal image of God, it is obvious that the church can find its best expression only at a personal level reflected in SCC. All other structures are created to support and foster the presence of the church in the modern world as exemplified in your SCC.

Don't put the cart before the horse. Your more vital experience of being church in SCC is the grassroots surge of life that will enable organizational levels of the church to reflect more faithfully the living Christ. Your pain and persistence in dealing with the unresponsiveness of others unites you to Christ in a special way. There is no greater love than to lay down your life for a friend, whether it be all at once or slowly over the minutes, hours, and days of a lifetime. Remember that this organized church with which you find fault has managed to keep the image of an espousal God alive through the centuries, making it available to you now. While you may find much to criticize, there is much more to be grateful for in the history of the church.

Q. SCC doesn't sound like a quick fix to solving the world's problems. Any short cuts?

A. After more than 30 years of working with SCCs, we believe we have tried every short cut. We are only now beginning to appreciate why after 2000 years of Christianity we are no further along than we are. Don't start with SCC if you are not ready for the long haul.

It's easy to think of God in espousal terms, but when you recognize that the implications of that image encompasses acceptance of yourself and your neighbor in an entirely new way, it becomes a different issue. There are lots of people who hate themselves not to mention their neighbor. An espousal relationship is the last thing many people want to hear about, let alone try. Good luck in announcing the good news of our espousal relationship with God! Many seem to prefer hearing only bad news.

Q. Is the main purpose of our SCC to feed the hungry, clothe the naked, visit the sick, give comfort to the afflicted and all the other corporal and spiritual works of mercy?

A. Healing is not the purpose of your SCC, but the visible proof that Christ is an accepted and active member of your gathering. The kingly servant characteristic is inseparable from an authentic SCC. Remember that your SCC cannot be "used" for anything no matter how worthy a cause, organization, or endeavor may be. Thus, your SCC cannot be "used" to build up the church because it is the church, that is, the presence of Christ in a particular time and place.

Your SCC is not to be used for fund raising, educating, or recruiting volunteers for soup kitchens, blood donations, hospital work or other worthy causes. While your SCC is an organization and may relate to various organization, its true reality is beyond organization because it constitutes the presence of Christ as priest, prophet, and kingly servant here and now. Your SCC exists for the sole purpose of bringing to maturity the believer who incorporates Christ as priest, prophet, and kingly servant in his or her daily life. Have no fear, when this happens all the needs of the world will be filled.

QUESTIONS FOR REVIEW AND DISCUSSION

1. The priest, prophet, and kingly servant characteristics of SCC are distinguishable in our minds but not in reality. What does this mean?

2. Should you feel guilty if your SCC is not sufficiently involved in social action or works of charity?

3. Why are we more inclined to look for sensational physical healing resulting from our SCC and less for inner healing?

Can you identify a healing that has taken place in you? In your SCC?

4. A SCC is like a healthy cell in a cancer-ridden body. What does this mean?

5. The kingly servant phenomenon is three dimensional. What does this mean? Why must each dimension be present to effect a healing? What is the Magnificat effect?

6. Why is befriending a stranger the most practical way of concretizing the kingly servant characteristic of your SCC? Why is it the best way of defining the relationship of your SCC to the local parish?

7. How can you distinguish between a true SCC and an imitation? Should you be concerned about proving the authenticity of your SCC?

8. In viewing modern society in general, it is obvious that kingly servant would be considered a contradiction in terms. What does this mean? Give examples?

9. Can you find the three dimensional kingly servant and the magnificat characteristics in other miracles of Christ as reported in the gospels? Explain.

10. Christ never performed a miracle to "prove" his divine mission but only to heal. Why? What application does this have to your SCC?

Chapter 7

The Honored Guest

You now know the way and you have the tools you need to fashion your SCC into a work of art infinitely surpassing the finest cathedral ever built with human hands. Your SCC is the house of God in which God, the chief architect, takes great delight; it is the bride setting forth with lamps burning bright to meet the divine spouse. We hope we have helped you open up a dialogue that leads to the discovery of a divine, long-suffering lover. It is time for us to step aside so that your own unique love story can unfold.

Before we do so, we want to explain two things. The first is that we know there is a good deal of repetition in these chapters. Since language cannot capture God's intimate love for you, we resorted to using repetition as a means for making our point.

Secondly, we hope you are not confused by the espousal image of God we have presented. Many have been raised with an image of God as an almighty creator or father who deserves our submission, thanks, and awe. An espousal image of God may offend the sense of reverence and respect that some feel should be emphasized in proper submission and obedience to God.

Indeed, it is no easy task to shift one's image of God because it is intimately bound up in how we perceive ourselves and the world around us. Therefore, new images of God have to be introduced slowly. As Christ admonished: It is not wise to put new wine in old wineskins, lest the container rupture and both old and new be lost (Matthew 9:17).

Thus, if your image of God is an authority figure, we urge you to be true to your own heart, while at the same time opening your mind and heart to whatever God wants to reveal to you. The writings in this book are not an attack on the old, but rather a challenge to build on old foundations in order that we might grow in faith.

What follows below is a sample "open" gathering at which members struggle with many of the concepts and insights we have introduced in this book. It's a gathering that we imagine taking place after members have worked and struggled for two years to become SCC. You are invited to sit in, listen, reflect, and learn, so that your SCC, too, will someday be a reflection of God.

The Gathering

We're on our own now after two years, and we have many unseen guests among us. So maybe the first order of business is to introduce ourselves and share what these past two years have meant to us. Since our gathering today is in my home, I think I should begin.

Julie My name is Julie. I'm the one who first invited Peter to join me to explore what SCC is all about. After Peter and I met for a year to develop the basic skills needed to enter into dialogue, we invited all of you to join us on our journey. Although these past two years have been difficult at times, looking back I can see the hand of God in my life. It was painful for me to put aside a childish faith and grow up into a mature faith, but the rewards for doing so makes the pain seem trivial now. I didn't discover this, however, until I had been through it. I have been Catholic all my life, but now after two years of experience with this SCC, I can truly say I understand my faith for the first time.

I had heard of SCC for years but never seemed to have the time to get involved. One day I just made up my mind that I was going to take the plunge. As I recall all this I can't adequately put my feelings into words, but what comes to mind is the parable of the mustard seed in the gospel. It is the smallest of seeds but it grows to be the largest herb, so that the birds of the air find shelter in its branches (Matthew 13:31). This SCC was like a very small seed sown in my busy world, and it has now become my greatest joy. I am so delighted that this joy has spread to you.

Peter I guess I should be next since I am a co-starter of this SCC with Julie. My name is Peter and I work for the city on a new waste-recycling project initiated three years ago. Julie asked me to join her to explore the possibilities of SCC and I guess she caught me at the right time. I was just getting into the promotion of recycling wastes, urged on by the realization that our dumps were nearly full and we would be buried in our own garbage if we didn't do something about it.

When Julie invited me, it occurred to me that we also throw too many people out as so much waste, and our streets are full of broken and homeless human beings. Since so many people today are strangers to one another, I thought maybe SCC would be a good way to recycle people back into community.

All of us here knew one another but were strangers in a way when we first came together. In our hectic world we don't take time to cultivate friendships. Now I feel I have the best friends I have ever had. This experience has made it clear to me that we can't just run over or cast away people we don't agree with. Each person is a precious pearl, but some are a little harder to open up than others. I believe we need to work at making a home that extends beyond blood to include others who are sincerely seeking. I view all of you as my real family.

Catherine My name is Catherine. I am retired, a widow, and all my children are married with families and lives of their own. I have enjoyed these gatherings because I am alone now and you all have become family to me, also. But, to be honest, I cannot connect with God in our gatherings. When I think of God, I think of the tabernacle at the parish church. When I want to talk to God or be in God's presence, I need to go over to the church. This SCC is all still very new to me.

Randy I would like to introduce myself and my wife, Alice. My name is Randy. Alice is a teacher and I work in construction as an architect. We have been married for 23 years. We hesitated about joining this gathering because we are both from large families and have four children of our own. All of our spare time is taken up with family activities. I must confess, however, the SCC has meant a great deal to us because we have rediscovered the excitement of talking to one another. We now share on a deeper level than we ever did before and I feel our marriage and family life have been greatly enhanced.

Alice I agree. However, our family often gets upset with the things we talk about. Some of them think we are losing our faith. We try to explain what goes on here, but we don't seem to get anywhere.

Ratia My name is Ratia. I am from India and am here on a scholarship to study engineering. I have been raised Hindu but have long been fascinated by the gospel. I jumped at the opportunity to join this SCC because I wanted to learn more about the meaning of the gospels.

What strikes me about our sharing is that growing closer to

God is seen as inseparable from growing closer to each other. This seems to be the central message of the gospels. In Hinduism it is just the opposite. To get close to God you must free yourself of your surroundings, including the people around you. In Hinduism the ideal is to use meditation to get outside yourself as a way of identifying with the mystery of life itself. This SCC makes me want to get to know myself better.

Gary My wife, Peg, and I are the only African-Americans in this SCC. We had to move to this area because I was transferred by my company. Both of us were raised Catholic and attended Catholic schools in Philadelphia, but we have given up on the institutional church. We find as African-Americans that it is hard, if not impossible, to fit into a white-dominated church. This experience with SCC has meant a lot to us. Now we feel that we can belong to a church that is racially blind and accepts us as persons.

Peg We had to do a lot of changing ourselves. We both had a lot of anger in us. Gary views the church as a white-dominated organization, but it is also male dominated, so it has been doubly difficult for me. But, as I have often pointed out, the church mirrors the society that forms it. We had to get over our anger so that we could take a fresh look at the gospels and bring a new spirit into the church. We must change the anger in ourselves before we can bring about change in the church. I am grateful for this SCC to help me turn around so that I can be a builder of a new church and not spend my life criticizing the old church.

Stan My name is Stan. I joined this SCC a few months after my divorce was final. This SCC has been a life saver to me. For a time I was completely lost, and I felt my life was over. During these past two years I have been able to find my way again. I am convinced that my wife and I would be married today if we had long ago been a part of this SCC to clear our vision of marriage, God, and the church. Neither of us knew what dialogue meant, let alone put it into practice. We just drifted apart, not even realizing what was happening. It puzzles me that the church would demand a lifetime commitment in marriage, which can only be achieved through dialogue, while it fosters a monologue in its parishes. Although I have been in this parish all my life, participation in this SCC is the first time I have ever been exposed to dialogue as central to my faith.

Mildred My name is Mildred and this is my husband, Joe. We have enjoyed the social aspects of our SCC these past two years. I don't want to offend anyone, but to be truthful we don't understand much of the discussion that goes on. We feel like Catherine: it's nice to get together and talk about spiritual things, but it is also very important to stay closely connected to our parish, pastor, Mass, and sacraments. We must avoid the danger of privatizing our spirituality and becoming divisive in the parish.

John I guess I'm last. I'm John. I don't belong to this parish but to a neighboring parish where I work as the coordinator of religious education. My pastor asked me to join your SCC to learn more about this new development with the idea of possibly introducing SCCs into our parish. I thought I knew all about ecclesiology, but the experience with this SCC has radically changed my image of the church. I had always thought of the church in terms of a trickle-down theory of grace, with grace flowing down from higher levels to those in need. Now, I see the church in terms of a bubble-up image where grace in the form of love beginning in our hearts bubbles up to envelop higher levels of the church and ultimately the whole world. I would like to take this occasion to thank all of you who have provided the love to allow me to sort through this upheaval in my own spiritual life.

Julie And thank you, John, for all you have contributed to the life of this SCC. You have helped us work through some tough issues. Now that we have finished with our introductions we must move on to general sharing about anything members want to bring up. Then we will share Scripture readings, and follow that with discussion, shared prayer, and our potluck supper. Let's start with general sharing. Does anyone have something to share?

Peg Yes, I ran across this article that reminded me of our SCC. It's called "Do We Have as Much Sense as a Goose?" and it's short, so I'll read it to you.

Next fall when you see geese heading south for the winter flying along in V formation, you might be interested in knowing what science has discovered about why they fly that way. It has been learned that as each bird flaps its wings, it creates an uplift for the bird immediately following. By flying in a V formation, the whole flock adds at least 71 percent greater flying range than if each bird flew on its own. (People who share a common direction and sense of community can get where they are going quicker and easier, because they are traveling on the thrust of one another.)

Whenever a goose falls out of formation, it suddenly feels the drag and resistance of trying to go it alone, and quickly gets back into formation to take advantage of the lifting power of the bird immediately in front. (If we have as much sense as a goose, we will stay in formation with those who are headed the same way we are going).

When the lead goose gets tired, it rotates back in the wing and another goose flies point. (It pays to take turns doing hard jobs, with people and with geese flying south.) The geese honk from behind to encourage those up front to keep up their speed. (What do we say when we honk from behind?)

Finally, when a goose gets sick, or is wounded by gunshot and falls out, two geese fall out of formation and follow it down to help and protect it. They stay with him until he is either able to fly or until he is dead, and then they launch out on their own or with another formation to catch up with their group. (If we have the sense of a goose we will stand by each other like that.)

Julie Thank you, Peg. I would love to have a copy of that. Is there anything else?

Peter We often speak of the world as a global village. A co-worker of mine translated worldwide statistics in terms of a hundred people. I found the statistics quite enlightening and would like to share my co-worker's report with you.

> If the world's population were represented by a village of a hundred people, it would consist of 56 Asians, 21 Europeans, 9 Africans, 8 South Americans, and 6 North Americans. Thirty of the people would be Christian, 17 Moslem, 13 Hindu, 5 Buddhist, 5 Animist, 9 miscellaneous, and 21 atheist or without religion. Of the 100 people, six would control half the total income, 50 would be hungry, 60 would live in shanty towns, and 70 would be illiterate.

Stan Reducing the five billion people on this planet down to a hundred helps me see where we stand a little better. I ran across some other revealing statistics in the October 21, 1991, issue of *U.S. News and World Report* and these statistics are: People who starve to death each year: 11 million; overweight U.S. adults: 34 million; money Americans spent eating out in 1980: $1.4 billion, in 1990: $1.6 billion; average calories consumed daily by North Americans: 3500, Africans: 2100; U.S. children under 12 who are regularly hungry: 5.5 million; percentage of food ads on Saturday morning TV for junk food: 95; average food-stamp allotment per meal: 50 cents; estimated catering bill for Elizabeth Taylor's eighth wedding: $300,000.

Alice Looking at the world through statistics like these from Peter and Stan only gives me a feeling of frustration. But breaking down the universal church into SCCs such as ours gives me hope and courage. I feel I can do something in SCC to make the church what I feel it ought to be. If enough people would do this, perhaps we could change some of those statistics.

Gary I was with a group of parishioners this past week when a new person joined us. I was introduced as one of the church people, referring to my membership in this SCC. I thought you would enjoy hearing how we are perceived by others. It was said, not in ridicule, but with an undertone of respect and interest.

John My pastor suggested that I ask my SCC if you would be willing to spend a day in retreat with him and the parish council members to talk about SCC. You might want to just think about it for now and we can discuss it after we reassemble following our potluck supper.

Liturgy Begins

Julie Anything further? Okay, then let's move on to our liturgy. In planning the liturgy for today I have chosen the theme of recognition. I would like our gathering today to be a special recognition of one of our members. As part of this recognition, you have noticed I have placed a reserved sign on the most comfortable chair in the room. The chair is reserved for a special recognition of one of our members.

Let us first prepare ourselves to give the special recognition by now reading the Scriptures for today. The readings are for next Sunday, the sixth Sunday of Easter. Mildred, would you please take the first reading; Ratia, would you take the second, and Gary, would you take the third?

Mildred The first reading is taken from Acts of the Apostles, chapter 10, verses 25-26, 34-35, and 44-48.

When Peter entered, Cornelius met him and fell down at his feet and worshipped him. But Peter lifted him up saying, "Stand up; I too am a human being." And Peter opened his mouth and said: "Truly I perceive that God shows no partiality, but in every nation anyone who is God-fearing and does what is right is acceptable to God."

While Peter was still saying this, the Holy Spirit fell on all who heard the word. And the believers from among the Jewish people who came with Peter were amazed, because the gift of the Holy Spirit had been poured out, even on the Gentiles. For they heard them speaking in tongues and extolling God. Then Peter declared, "Can anyone forbid water for baptizing these people who have received the Holy Spirit just as we have?" And Peter commanded them to be baptized in the name of Jesus Christ. And they asked him to remain for some days.

Ratia The second reading is taken from the first letter of John, chapter 4, verses 7-10.

Beloved, let us love one another; for love is of God, and everyone who loves is born of God and knows God. One who does not love does not know God, for God is love. In this the love of God was made manifest among us, that God sent into the world God's only Son, so that we might live through him. Love consists in this: not that we have loved God but that has God loved us and sent the Son to be the expiation for our sins.

Gary The third reading is taken from the gospel of John, chapter 15, verses 9-17.

At that time Jesus said, "As the Father has loved me, so have I loved you; abide in my love. If you keep my commandments, you will abide in my love, just as I have kept my Father's commandments and abide in my Father's love. These things I have spoken to you, that my joy may be in you, and that your joy may be full. "This is my commandment, that you love one another as I have loved you. Greater love has no one than this, that a man lay down his life for his friends. You are my friends if you do what I command you. No longer do I call you servants, for servants do not know what their master is doing; but I have called you friends, for all that I have heard from my Father I have made known to you. You did not choose me, but I chose you and appointed you that you should go and bear fruit and that your fruit should abide; so that whatever you ask the Father in my name, the Father may give it to you. This I command you, to love one another."

Julie Thank you, Mildred, Ratia, and Gary. Does anyone have any thoughts to share about the readings?

Ratia It seems strange to me that the Holy Spirit came upon the Gentile Cornelius even before he was baptized. I have always thought that the grace of the Holy Spirit came at baptism and at confirmation.

Stan Also, Cornelius is baptized without previous preparation or instructions.

Peter Times were different back in those days. We live in much more complex times. It is so much easier today for people to be misled. Without guidance from the church, who knows where we would end up!

Gary What I get out of the readings is that Christ wants us to love one another whether we are black or white, Jew or Gentile, Hindu or Christian. It seems to me that is exactly what a small community such as this is all about.

John Gary, it's easy to talk about love; words are cheap. How do we really get at the meaning of love?

Gary I guess each has to answer that question for himself

or herself. I know that Peg and I were turned off by the prejudice and racism we experienced in a white society and even in
the church. We had to swallow our pride along with a lot of
hurt when we decided to join this all-white group. It may not
seem much, but we stuck out our necks again not knowing
what would happen. Maybe, in some small way, this is the
meaning of love.

Peter Gary has a good point. Each of us must answer for
ourselves what love is in practice. Our answer will change
over time and come closer to the answer of Christ who laid
down his life for his friends.

Stan I gave up going on a fishing trip with my buddies to
be here today. Again, it's not much, but I think all of us who
make an effort to be here every time at our gathering are lay-
ing down our lives little by little for each other rather than all
at once as did Jesus.

Mildred I would like to go back to the apology made by
our SCC guides before they left, regarding changing our image
of God. I don't understand this business about images.

Randy The way I see it, it's like having a blueprint for a
building I am going to construct. When I see the blueprint, I
am able to see in my mind what the building will look like
even before the first shovel of dirt is turned. In constructing
our vision of God we need a blueprint. For example, Ratia
needs a blueprint that reflects a Hindu's belief that God is
identified with life. As far as we are concerned, because we believe God to be our heavenly Father, we try to create father images. Thus, the delegate of God is called "pope," another word
for father. The pope appoints bishops, a word that implies eld-
ers, or fathers. The bishops appoint pastors whom we address
as father. This hierarchy of fathers serves as a blueprint to help
us see God as a heavenly Father.

SCC is also a blueprint, but it is designed to help us see
God and our relationships in the church in espousal terms
rather than in a father-son or shepherd-sheep image. Today's

Scripture readings tell us that God is the kind of love that produces friends, not a parent-child relationship. These Scripture readings are talking about an espousal image. I come to each meeting of our SCC because I like the SCC as my blueprint for imaging God as love. When I say I rediscovered how interesting Alice is, I mean I don't take her for granted any more as I used to. I now connect the love between Alice and myself with the love between God and me because of what I have learned in this SCC. Each day I try to grow in my espousal perception of God as I grow in an espousal relationship with Alice.

Alice Randy, you make a good point about love. Genuine love can only exist between equals and that is why we have such a short supply of it in the world today. For example, I've noticed that people try to be friends with their children when their children are kids, and parents to them when their kids are grown adults. Rarely do you find parents as friends with their grown children based on equality. I read recently where a 92-year-old man referred to his 67-year-old son as his kid. It's hard to be friends adult-to-adult as Jesus was.

Peg Ratia, what would be an example of a blueprint for a Hindu to reach God?

Ratia Meditation is the classic blueprint for Hindus in their efforts to touch God. In meditation Hindus try to remove themselves from all sense contact with the outside world and even escape from his own individual existence in an effort to be absorbed into pure life. A meditation may last for hours or days. For some it can last a lifetime. Trappist monks in this country are closest to following the ideal blueprint for reaching God, in the mind of a Hindu.

Mildred I thought we were forbidden by the first commandment from forming an image, or blueprint, as you say, of God. Imaging God is idolatry!

John It is impossible for us to even think without using images. Images are to the mind what food is to the body. If we did not have an image of God, it would mean we would never think about God. The first commandment forbids us to make a final image of God, lest we end up worshipping the image instead of God. In other words, we are supposed to develop more mature images of God as we grow in faith.

John In Old Testament times the Jews developed a rigid tribal image of their relationship with God and ended up worshipping the religious laws that were meant to hold their tribe together; they somehow lost touch with their divine chieftain. As reflected in today's readings, Jesus introduced an espousal image of God in that rigid atmosphere. As you know, it was difficult for the Jews to shift from a familiar tribal blueprint to an espousal image defined by personal dialogue. We must not repeat the same mistake by shutting out a better image of God in our lives. There may be better images, or blueprints, in the future to put us in touch with God, but right now I think an espousal one is undoubtedly the best for me.

Randy We are always working over blueprints in order to construct a building that in the end is more functional, environmentally sound, safer, and more aesthetic. I guess we forget all of us live our lives consciously or unconsciously based on a blueprint, known only to ourselves. If we modify blueprints for better buildings, it makes a lot of sense to me to refine the blueprints that govern how we live our lifes.

Peg Does everyone have to subscribe to the same image of God?

Randy I don't think so. I suspect Ratia favors a vital image of God and therefore stresses meditation. Mildred seems to like a tribal image and therefore often speaks of the need for linkage with organized religion, and John has discovered an espousal image and now finds SCC central to pursuing that perception of God. In practice, I think people try to blend together various images of God but invariably one image will dominate over all the others.

But, as Peter mentioned earlier, I don't think we should throw people away because they do not have the same blueprint as we do. I feel we need people with emphases on different images of God to give our SCC a greater vitality. God is so far beyond our comprehension that we need one another to give witness to how God is present in another person's life in order to get a clearer understanding of how God is present in our own.

Mildred How do I change my so-called blueprint of God or life?

John Slowly, laboriously, and sometimes painfully. Just coming to this SCC is inducing a change from a tribal to an espousal image of God, and therefore of the church. I have been in religious education for years, but it was not until I experienced the love in this SCC that I was able to shift my image of the church from a trickle-down to a bubble-up source of grace and love. I wouldn't miss one of these meetings for the world. Randy is right: I personally need SCC to redesign my blueprint, so to speak. Coming here to experience this SCC is how I can bring change to the images that control my life.

Mildred I am not sure that our pastor and bishop are going to like this; it sounds like anarchy.

John Genuine love is not anarchy but the highest form of order. As far as the pastor and bishop are concerned, remember that Vatican II spoke of the church first and foremost as a community. Typically it may take a hundred years before the full impact of a universal council reaches the grassroots level. Our pastors and bishops must move slowly because people in general move very slowly. This doesn't mean that we who love the church can't move ahead. Our church leaders will follow when they see people ready to move.

Catherine It seems to me that if our pastor subdivides the parish into SCCs and appoints a leader for each, then the tribal image of the church would only be greatly increased!

John I agree, but only if spiritual or psychological force is used. We must not force people into SCCs by playing on fear of losing their souls or some punishment. Even to suggest that

Christ would be displeased if we didn't join SCC is inappropriate. If people come out of fear, it would destroy SCC. All of us
are here freely of our own choosing, aren't we? It has to be like
this for all SCCs. Love is the only basis for our gathering in the
name of Christ. Where love is, there is God. We just read that
in the Scriptures.

Gary In Communist countries people were forced into
small neighborhood groups for indoctrination. The disastrous
results in Russia and Eastern Europe today is there for the
whole world to see. Obviously, force and fear have no place as
the basis for human society, let alone for the church.

Mildred Well, if the pastor doesn't appoint leaders for
SCCs, who is supposed to lead?

Peg My understanding of chapter five is that true leadership is prophetic. The one who points the way toward greater
unity is in fact the true leader. Christ is our leader precisely because he points toward an espousal union with God as the
only basis of unity for all of humanity. This is God's plan from
the very beginning. Thus, whoever among us moves us toward espousal relationship is fulfilling a prophetic leadership
role.

Peter That makes sense to me. If Julie didn't resolve in her
heart that SCC was a practical way to find God, she would
never have contacted me and what we all feel today would not
have happened. To me, Julie is a prophetic leader.

John I would like to make another observation. In today's
reading Jesus makes a point in telling his disciples that they
are not servants but friends because he opens his heart to
them. I think that is precisely what we are trying to do with
each other. That is why I now have, as I mentioned earlier, a
bubble-up image for the church. It makes a lot of sense for us
to be a small community so that we can know each other and
be friends as we share what is important to each of us. The
love that we find will bubble-up and renew the parish and ultimately the whole community.

Alice John, you keep bringing up that bubble-up image of the church. It must affect you a great deal.

John My image of God and, therefore, of the church has been turned upside down. I can't begin to put into words what this does to me. I find myself picking up the gospels and reading them as if for the first time. I now understand the gospels in a way that I never dreamed possible. I can't quite put my finger on it, but it seems like I have recovered the sense of wonder as a little child, making it possible to understand Scriptures in a way scholars might easily miss.

Mildred What do you mean?

John It is hard to explain. All the world is based on tribal images. We have democracy in this country, but in practice our country is more tribal than democratic because it is often those higher up on the hierarchy of wealth or education that are heard, while the poor become nearly invisible. This SCC is the first time in my life where I have glimpsed the possibility of a whole new order for the world based on love and not tribal affiliation. That excites me very much but it's going to take a lot of time for me to sort out the ramifications.

Peter It sounds like exaggerated individualism to me.

John Only if you think of individual in isolated rather than relational terms.

Peter I don't understand, John. Would you give an example?

John Sure. Individuals marry but, in a good marriage, the couple do not give up their individuality; rather, the love relationship between the couple enhances the unique individuality of both spouses. The same is true here in our SCC. The love that draws us together does not suppress but increases the revelation of the unique personality of each individual. Joe here hasn't said a word, but that's okay. He's here every week and that says a lot. Each person is free to be himself or herself, and all are equally received. The sense of community that we all feel is the presence of a loving God. By remaining faithful to our true selves we facilitate the revelation of God as the mystery of love that unites us.

But I think we're drifting away from the theme of our liturgy today. Before we go any further, I would like to ask Julie which member she has chosen to occupy that comfortable chair as a way of special recognition?

Julie Let's hear from you. Whom do you think should receive special recognition?

Peter I think it should be Peg or Gary. I must admit, I really didn't understand the pain African-Americans felt until I met Peg and Gary and shared with them for the past two years. Our recognition would repay in some small way the anguish they have experienced so many times in their lives.

Mildred I think we should recognize John. He is making a concerted effort to spread SCCs and to insure that they are tied into the parish. We'll get lost if we don't stay linked to the pastor.

Ratia Julie, do you have a particular member in mind? If so, can you give us a hint?

Julie Yes, I have one member in mind and this person has never missed a meeting.

Stan Most of us have been at every meeting but Catherine always manages to be among the earliest arrivals and stays for clean-up. Is it Catherine?

Catherine I think it might be the Holy Spirit.

Randy Wait a minute, Peter, you and Julie met long before the rest of us. I bet Julie has it in mind to recognize your efforts.

Mildred Julie, we give up. Which member have you chosen to recognize?

Julie Each time we come together we recognize one another and in so doing have grown to know and love one another. Each time we come together a member of our SCC has been present but no chair has been offered. Yet, without his presence we would not be here together. I wish to recognize the presence of Jesus, the beloved of God, at our gathering in a special way today. The chair is for him.

We are all familiar with the presence of Christ in the tabernacle in the parish church, but we forget he is there because he is first of all here in our church. To give recognition to Christ's presence here as a very important member of this SCC, let us all stand and gather around this table in the center of the room on which I have placed a burning candle, a symbol of the risen Christ.

Julie (handing each member an unlighted candle) We draw our life from Christ, the light of the world. I would like each of you to reach out with your candle and light it from the burning candle representing the presence of Christ and while doing so express a prayer of thanksgiving for the presence of Christ and for one of the members of our SCC, each of whom are drawn here by Christ and are a special gift to us all. Your prayer may be silent or shared with the community.

Let us conclude our celebration by giving to each other an embrace of peace. Then we'll continue our celebration by gathering around the table for our potluck supper.

(The supper is enjoyed by all, along with lively conversation.)

Concluding Gathering

Julie John brought up the issue of going on a retreat with his pastor and parish council members. What is your pleasure?

Mildred I think it's an excellent idea. We'll get a chance to explain what SCC is all about to the pastor and parish leaders. That is where SCC must begin. They will then know what they are trying to set up in the parish and there will be less danger of splinter groups if the pastor is actively involved.

Peg Gary and I will need to know well in advance because we have a lot of things going on.

Stan It sounds good to me, but we should pick a time when we can all be there. We will need everyone because I understand there are 14 members of the parish council plus the pastor.

Julie From looking at the nodding heads, I guess we are in favor of the proposal.

Ratia Hold on a minute. With 14 council members, a pastor, and 12 of us...that makes 27 people. You can't have dialogue in that large a group because only the loudest people will be heard. It has taken us two years to get as far as we are and we still have a long way to go.

I suggest we invite John's pastor and one council member to come to our gatherings for awhile and encourage them to start SCC like Julie and Peter did originally. Then the pastor and at least one parish leader will have a better vision of what they are asking parishioners to do. It is easy to organize parishes into SCCs but to become SCC is a lifetime of struggle. Maybe two of the members of our SCC would be willing to start SCC in John's parish at the same time. I am very leery of well meaning people jumping into SCC and then start looking for short cuts.

Julie Ratia has a good point. Looking back over the struggle I had to get started with myself, let alone with Peter, and then with all of you, inclines me to accept Ratia's point. We really can't explain the experience of communion that we feel. If you agree, we can ask John to invite his pastor and a parish leader to our next few meetings.

Since you all seem to be in agreement that this is a wiser course to take, we'll move on. The next item of business is to designate who will host the next meeting, including planning the liturgy and assigning what each member should bring for the potluck supper.

Ratia It's my turn to host our gathering. You are all more than welcome at my apartment. I know some of you are a little uncomfortable because of my Hindu background. I must confess that I find it difficult to relate to Christians in a tribal sense. When I learned that "Christian" may be related to the

Greek word for "beloved," I felt much better because I can identify with an espousal image of God. I wish we could all refer to each other using "beloved" instead of "Christian." If we did this, I think some would not be so uncomfortable with my Hindu background.

John I think we have all learned a lot from you, Ratia. You have introduced an element of reflection to our SCC that we never would have had without you. I know who I am now much more than ever before as a result of a habit of reflection that I have learned from you.

Julie I agree with John and I am going to suggest we make reflection a formal part of our gatherings from now on by agreeing on a question about ourselves, reflecting on it, and sharing our reflections at the next meeting. For example, "What is your earliest memory?" Each should reflect on this and then each can share with the community at our next gathering the earliest memory of his or her life. Then at the next meeting we can come up with another question to reflect on. For example, "What have others told us about our early childhood that we were too young to remember ourselves?" or "What is your earliest impression of your parents?" and so on.

Peg I think that's an excellent idea, Julie. My early years were very hard years and the reflecting could be very healing for me.

John I think it is even more significant than that. We all were raised with the idea that doctrine is more important than people. If I have understood anything about this SCC it is that to know God I must know myself, and if I am to know myself I must know each of you in this community. The whole purpose of our SCC is to know real people, myself included, in order to know a real God. When we say that God became flesh, it seems to me to be saying that to find God we need to find each other, not just formulate some abstract doctrines.

Stan I belonged to the same parish for over thirty years and never really knew anyone. Mass on Sunday, sacraments, contributions—that was about all there was to my understanding.

Julie I see heads nodding in agreement and I take this to mean that each meeting from now on we will focus on some very specific element in our lives, the more specific the better, then reflect on it and when we gather share our reflections or recollections with the community.

I think also we can take to heart what Ratia has called to our attention regarding the use of the word Christian. Whenever we hear or use the term from now on we can translate it in our own minds to the word "beloved." It will help us realize that all people are beloved of God whether they are aware of it or not. Besides, how will people become aware of it unless we start thinking and treating them as God's beloved?

The conversation among members continues unabated. Julie pauses, looks at her watch and sees that the meeting has already lasted over four hours and shows no signs of ending soon. She looks at the reserved sign on the chair, the burning candle, and the excitement of the little community. She thinks to herself, "Indeed, Christ is risen. He is here as our honored guest! My soul magnifies the Lord, and my spirit rejoices in God my savior."